D
F
LIB
4 AL

2
28

2

PHOTOGRAPHER'S
POCKET BOOK

PHOTOGRAPHER'S POCKET BOOK

Edited by

CARLTON WALLACE

LONDON
EVANS BROTHERS LIMITED

First Published 1953

3, B180553

CONTENTS

Part One

CAMERAS AND ACCESSORIES

Part Two

EXPOSURE

Part Three

THE DARKROOM

Part Four
LANTERN SLIDES

Part Five
SUB-STANDARD CINÉ

Part Six
COLOUR PHOTOGRAPHY

LIST OF ILLUSTRATIONS

Part One

CAMERAS AND ACCESSORIES

CAMERA DATA

THE NUMBER of different makes, types and sizes of cameras is so great that something can readily be found for any purpose. In this pocket book no attempt has been made to deal with the kind of camera which is of interest only to the research specialist, however; he will be in touch with sources of information concerning his apparatus already. The cameras described here will be, in the main, for general, press and field use.

Types of Camera

From time to time there are fashions in cameras. For example, there is the "miniature," the instrument using 35-mm. film of the ciné type, which has a very large following, despite the high cost of precision products. But the term "miniature" has no exact significance, for it has been applied not only to 35-mm. apparatus, but also to all cameras which produce negatives up to $2\frac{1}{4}$ in. square. Since, however, the tendency now is to keep down the cost of making negatives on film by limiting the manufacture of roll films, or at least of cameras taking roll film, to smaller sizes, it is felt that the term "miniature" is rapidly becoming of limited usefulness.

On the whole, photography at nearly all levels now tends towards the small negative, varying degrees of fine-grain development, contact prints for general examination of results, and enlargements for the finished product. Only where extensive retouching of the negative is still necessary, despite greatly advanced techniques of lighting and processing, are the larger sizes still favoured.

By far the greater number of cameras made are for roll film in four sizes: 35-mm. and sizes 88, 27 and 20. For the worker who wishes to be able to process single negatives there are also plate cameras (which, with adaptation, will take cut film and, in some cases, roll film as well). Some older roll-film cameras take the sizes 116 and 118, but as these cameras cease to have useful life, it seems likely that the manufacture of the 116- and 118-size films will eventually cease.

Sizes of roll film and of other types of negative material will be found on pages 56 and 57.

Lists of Cameras

In the lists of cameras which appear on pages 14 to 17, no attempt has been made to be comprehensive. Some forty film cameras have been shown, plus a few press and technical instruments, the whole covering a wide field of usefulness and price. The selection has been independent and impersonal.

Of necessity, a certain number of abbreviations have been used, and a guide to these is to be found at the end of the roll-film camera table.

LENSES

THE PURPOSE of a camera lens is to bring together the light rays from an image being photographed and to direct them evenly on to the surface of negative material. Strictly the word "lens" applies to a single piece of glass shaped for the above purpose, but in practice the word is applied also to a number of such glasses acting together and fixed together in a single mount. It is in the second sense that the word "lens" is used throughout this book.

It is common knowledge that a lens is not strictly necessary for the transfer of an image on to negative material; a pinhole in one side of a light-tight box will also effect the transfer. A pinhole is extremely slow, however, and lenses must be used in order to make photography effectively "instantaneous."

Types of Standard Lenses

Types of lenses can be varied according to the purposes for which they are to be used, and (more restrictedly) according to cost.

Mensicus Lenses are single glasses ground to concavo-convex shape, or cast to that shape in clear plastic material. They are cheap, and hence are found in inexpensive cameras. They cannot work at large apertures owing to distortion of the image at the limits of the picture, and are generally mounted in box cameras, working at fixed focus at between *f.* 11 and *f.* 16

Achromats. Some of the defects of the mensicus lens can be overcome by cementing together two glasses of slightly different characteristics so that they become, for all practical purposes, a single glass. Such double lenses are known as achromats. Maximum aperture, about *f.* 11.

Rapid Rectilinear (*R.R.*). The mounting of two achromats to act as a single lens reduces further the defects mentioned above; such a lens is known as a rapid rectilinear. It will work at a somewhat larger aperture (about *f.* 8 is the limit), and will provide the facility of variable focus. The rapid rectilinear is generally to be found on cheap folding cameras.

Anastigmat. Problems of distortion of various kinds are overcome by mounting a number of glasses together so that each glass corrects the defects of one or more others. Such a lens is given the name anastigmat, and it is the type which is fitted to all cameras used for serious work and which are not of specialist character (e.g. designed for portraiture only). It can work at very large apertures—to about *f.* 1·5 in precision cameras—with full focusing facilities.

Special Lenses

The anastigmat lens fitted to a camera as standard is a general-purpose lens, intended for average use. As fitted to the general run of cameras, it will have an angle of acceptance of about 45° or 50° (that is, it will cover an image 22½° to 25° each side of the centre-line of the camera) and will focus from about 4 or 5 ft. to infinity.

(*Continued on page* 18)

35 mm. and Roll-Film Cameras

Size	*Name*	*Negative size*	*No. of exp.*	*Lens*
35 mm.	Baldinette (F)	24×36 mm.	36	Radionar *f.* 3·5
	Contaflex	24×36 mm.	36	Various to *f.* 1·5
	Contax IIIA	24×36 mm.	36	Various to *f.* 1·5
	Elca II	24×24 mm.	50	Elocar *f.* 3·5
	Finetta IVD	24×36 mm.	36	Finetar *f.* 4
	Ikonta (F)	24×36 mm.	36	Various to *f.* 2·8
	Iloca IIa	24×36 mm.	36	Ilitar *f.* 3·5
	Karat I (F)	24×36 mm.	12	Solinar *f.* 3·5
	Leica IIIA	24×36 mm.	36	Various to *f.* 1·5
	Rectaflex	24×36 mm.	36	Xenon *f.* 2
	Reid	24×36 mm.	36	THC *f.* 2
	Retina I (F)	24×36 mm.	36	Various *f.* 3·5
	Wrayflex	24×32 mm.	45	Various to *f.* 2
88 . .	Coronet Cub	28×40 mm.	8	About *f.* 11
27 . .	Brownie Reflex (B)	$1\frac{5}{8}\times1\frac{5}{8}$ in.	12	About *f.* 11
	Comet	$1\frac{1}{8}\times1\frac{5}{8}$ in.	16	About *f.* 11
	Purma Plus	$1\frac{1}{4}\times1\frac{1}{4}$ in.	16	*f.* 6·3
	Rondine B (B)	$1\frac{5}{8}\times2\frac{1}{2}$ in.	8	Ferrania *f.* 11
20 & 62	Agiflex II	$2\frac{1}{4}\times2\frac{1}{4}$ in.	12	Agilux *f.* 3·5
	Agifold I (F)	$2\frac{1}{4}\times2\frac{1}{4}$ in.	12	Agilux *f.* 4·5
	Agifold II (F)	$2\frac{1}{4}\times2\frac{1}{4}$ in.	12	Agilux *f.* 4·5
	Baldalux (F)	$2\frac{1}{4}\times3\frac{1}{4}$ in.	8*	Radionar *f* 4·5
	Baldix (F)	$2\frac{1}{4}\times2\frac{1}{4}$ in.	12	Ennagon *f.* 3·5
	Box-Tengor (B)	$2\frac{1}{4}\times3\frac{1}{4}$ in.	8	Frontar *f.* 9
	Brownie Six-20 (F)	$2\frac{1}{4}\times3\frac{1}{4}$ in.	8	Anaston *f.* 6·3
	Conway (B)	$2\frac{1}{4}\times3\frac{1}{4}$ in.	8	About *f.* 11
	Coronet 12-20 (B)	$2\frac{1}{4}\times2\frac{1}{4}$ in.	12	About *f.* 11
	Craftsman (B)	$2\frac{1}{4}\times2\frac{1}{4}$ in.	12	*f.* 9
	Curlew III (F)	$2\frac{1}{4}\times3\frac{1}{4}$ in.	8	Roytal *f.* 4·5
	Duaflex (B)	$2\frac{1}{4}\times2\frac{1}{4}$ in.	12	About *f.* 11
	Elioflex (B)	$2\frac{1}{4}\times2\frac{1}{4}$ in.	12	Galileo *f.* 8
	Fulvue (B)	$2\frac{1}{4}\times2\frac{1}{4}$ in.	12	About *f.* 11
	Isolette V (F)	$2\frac{1}{4}\times2\frac{1}{4}$ in.	12	Agnar *f.* 4·5
	King Penguin (F)	$2\frac{1}{4}\times3\frac{1}{4}$ in.	8	*f.* 11
	Nettar II (F)	$2\frac{1}{4}\times2\frac{1}{4}$ in.	12	Novar *f.* 4·5
	Ranger II	$2\frac{1}{4}\times3\frac{1}{4}$ in.	8	Ensar *f.* 6·3
	Rolleiflex Automat	$2\frac{1}{4}\times2\frac{1}{4}$ in.	12	Tessar *f.* 3·5
	Selfix 12/20 (F)	$2\frac{1}{4}\times2\frac{1}{4}$ in.	12	Xpres *f.* 3·5
	Selfix 16/20 (F)	$1\frac{5}{8}\times2\frac{1}{4}$ in.	16	Ensar *f.* 4·5
	Semflex Otomatic	$2\frac{1}{4}\times2\frac{1}{4}$ in.	12	Berthiot *f.* 3·5

* *with mask for* 16 *negatives at* $1\frac{5}{8}\times2\frac{1}{4}$ *in.*

Key to Abbreviations:

Name: (B)=Box Camera; (F)=Folding (bellows) camera.

Lens: Int. Lens=Interchangeable Lens, as distinct from supplementary—"portrait attachment"—lens.

Shutter (Type): F/P=focal plane; Beh. Lens=behind-lens shutter, but not of focal-plane type; B=bulb; T=time; I=instantaneous. A figure after B or T indicates no. of instantaneous speeds.

Shutter (Other Details): Del. act.=delayed-action mechanism; Fl. syn.=

Int. Lens	Type	Shutter					R/F	V/F	P/R
		Range	Del. act.	Fl. syn.	B/R	D/E prev.			
	Prontor SV	$1-\frac{1}{300}$	Yes	Yes	Yes	Yes		Opt.	III
Yes	F/P	$\frac{1}{2}-\frac{1}{1000}$	Yes	Yes	Yes	Yes		Refl.	V
Yes	F/P	$\frac{1}{2}-\frac{1}{1000}$	Yes	Yes	Yes	Yes	Yes	Opt.	V
	Pronto	$\frac{1}{25}-\frac{1}{200}$	Yes	Yes	Yes	Yes		Opt.	III
Yes	Beh. Lens	$\frac{1}{25}-\frac{1}{100}$	Yes	Yes	Yes	Yes		Opt.	II
	Compur R	$1-\frac{1}{500}$		Yes	Yes	Yes		Opt.	III
	Prontor SV	$1-\frac{1}{300}$	Yes	Yes	Yes	Yes	Yes	Opt.	IV
	Compur R	$1-\frac{1}{500}$		Yes	Yes	Yes		Opt.	III
Yes	F/P	$\frac{1}{2}-\frac{1}{1000}$	Yes	Yes	Yes	Yes	Yes	Opt.	V
Yes	F/P	$1-\frac{1}{1000}$	Yes	Yes	Yes	Yes		Refl.	V
Yes	F/P	$1-\frac{1}{1000}$		Yes	Yes	Yes	Yes	Opt.	V
	Compur R	$1-\frac{1}{500}$		Yes	Yes	Yes		Opt.	III
Yes	F/P	$\frac{1}{2}-\frac{1}{1000}$		Yes	Yes	Yes		Refl.	V
	T & I	Abt. $\frac{1}{25}$		Yes				Opt.	I
	B & I	Abt. $\frac{1}{25}$		Yes	Yes			Br.	I
	B & I	Abt. $\frac{1}{25}$		Yes	Yes			Opt.	I
	F/P	$\frac{1}{25}-\frac{1}{500}$		Yes	Yes			Opt.	II
	T & I	Abt. $\frac{1}{25}$		Yes				Br. & Fr.	I
Yes	F/P	$2-\frac{1}{500}$		Yes	Yes	Yes		Refl. & Opt.	V
	Agilux 4	$\frac{1}{25}-\frac{1}{125}$		Yes	Yes	Yes		Opt. & Br.	III
	Agilux 8	$1-\frac{1}{150}$		Yes	Yes	Yes	Yes*	Opt.	III
	Prontor S	$1-\frac{1}{300}$	Yes	Yes	Yes	Yes		Opt.	III
	Prontor SV	$1-\frac{1}{300}$	Yes	Yes	Yes	Yes		Opt.	III
	T & I	Abt. $\frac{1}{25}$		Yes	Yes	Yes		Opt.	II
	B T & 2	$\frac{1}{25}$ & $\frac{1}{50}$		Yes				Br.	II
	T & I	Abt. $\frac{1}{25}$		Yes		Yes		Opt.	II
	T & I	Abt. $\frac{1}{25}$		Yes				Br.	I
	B & 2	$\frac{1}{25}$ & $\frac{1}{75}$		Yes	Yes			Br.	II
	Epsilon 4	$\frac{1}{25}-\frac{1}{350}$		Yes	Yes	Yes		Opt.	III
	B & I	Abt. $\frac{1}{25}$		Yes	Yes			Br.	I
	B & 4	$\frac{1}{25}-\frac{1}{200}$		Yes	Yes			Br. & Fr.	I
	T & I	Abt. $\frac{1}{25}$		Yes				Br.	I
	Pronto	$\frac{1}{25}-\frac{1}{200}$	Yes	Yes	Yes			Opt.	III
	B & I	Abt. $\frac{1}{25}$		Yes				Fr.	I
	Pronto	$\frac{1}{25}-\frac{1}{200}$	Yes	Yes	Yes			Opt.	III
	Trikon	$\frac{1}{25}-\frac{1}{100}$		Yes				Fr.	II
	Compur R	$1-\frac{1}{500}$		Yes	Yes	Yes		Refl.	V
	Epsilon 8	$1-\frac{1}{800}$		Yes	Yes	Yes		Opt.	III
	Epsilon 8	$1-\frac{1}{300}$		Yes	Yes	Yes		Opt.	III
	Orec F	$1-\frac{1}{400}$		Yes				Refl. & Fr.	IV

* and built-in exposure meter.

synchronised for flash; B/R=body-release; D/E prev.=double-exposure prevention mechanism.

Rangefinder=R/F.

Viewfinder (=V/F): Br.=Brilliant (i.e. of the reflex type, of any size, but not coupled to the taking lens for focusing); Fr.=open frame finder; Opt.=direct-vision optical finder; Refl.=reflex finder, coupled to taking lens for focus, or using taking lens.

Price Range (=P/R): I=up to about £5; II=from about £5 up to about £15; III=£15 to £35; IV=£35 to £70; V=above £70.

Press and Technical Cameras

The twelve cameras in the following selected list cannot be tabulated so readily as the roll-film cameras mentioned earlier, and each is therefore separately described.

Dawe Electronic Press. Size: 5×4 in. with adaptation to 9×12 cm. and $\frac{1}{4}$-plate; plate or cut film. *Lens:* 13·5 cm., *f*.4·5; interchangeable. *Shutters:* focal plane to $\frac{1}{1000}$ sec., and MX Compur Rapid, synchronised and with delayed action, 9 speeds. *Viewfinder:* open frame. *Rangefinder:* coupled long base, 3 ft. to inf. *Special Features:* illuminated distance scale and focus-spot for night photography, with built-in batteries; specially adapted for use with electronic flash, but takes ordinary flash bulbs.

Linhof Technika. Sizes: 6×9 cm., 9×12 cm, 13×18 cm., 5×4 in., 7×5 in.; plate, etc. *Lens:* sixteen available, according to requirements. *Shutters:* according to lens selected. *Viewfinder:* Universal. *Rangefinder:* coupled, for most models. *Special Features:* folding body, drop baseboard, rack and pinion focusing; triple extension; rise, cross and swing front; revolve and tilt back; roll-film adaptor.

Makina III Press. Size: $3\frac{1}{2} \times 2\frac{1}{2}$; plate, with roll-film and film-pack adaptors. *Lenses:* Plaubel Anticomar 10 cm., *f*.4·2 or *f*.2·9; Telemakinar 19 cm., *f*.4·8; Orthor 7·3 cm., *f*.6·8. *Shutter:* Compur, 8 speeds to $\frac{1}{200}$, with delayed action and synchronised. *Viewfinders:* open frame, and direct-vision optical. *Rangefinder:* coupled 3 ft. to inf.

Micro-Press. Size: 5×4 in.; plate, etc. *Lenses:* various, interchangeable with between-lens shutters. *Shutters:* focal plane to $\frac{1}{1000}$ sec., synchronised; and shutters with lenses. *Viewfinder:* open frame. *Rangefinder:* coupled, with interchangeable cam plates to suit lenses. *Special Features:* double extension; rise, cross and tilt front.

Micro-Technical VI. Size: 5×4 in.; plate, etc. General features as for Micro-Press, but with triple extension, rotating back and swing front.

Minex. *Sizes:* $3\frac{1}{2} \times 2\frac{1}{2}$ in., $\frac{1}{4}$-plate and 5×4 in.; plate, etc. *Lens:* according to requirements. *Shutter:* focal plane, speeds $\frac{1}{8}$ to $\frac{1}{1000}$. *Viewfinder:* focusing screen. *Special features:* double extension, revolving back, rise and fall front; body in teak and brass or morocco covered.

P.I.M. Monorail Technical. *Sizes:* 5×4 in., $\frac{1}{2}$-plate, whole-plate, 10×8 in.; plate, etc. *Lens:* interchangeable, with bayonet fitting. *Special features:* square bellows, $2\frac{1}{4}$-in. rise or drop front, 30° horizontal swing, 35° vertical swing, $2\frac{1}{2}$-in. cross front. A laboratory camera with the widest possibilities for adaptation.

Plaubel Peco Technical. *Size:* 5×4 in.; plate, etc. A monorail camera of characteristics similar to the P.I.M., but with an exceptionally large lens mount.

Sinar Monorail Technical. *Size:* 5×4 in.; plate, etc. Another camera of characteristics similar to the P.I.M., with a range of lenses from $2\frac{1}{2}$ to 20 in. focal length interchangeable by removable panels, and self-cocking synchronised shutter.

Universal Press. *Size:* 5×4 in.; plate, etc. *Lenses:* various, interchangeable. *Shutters:* focal plane to $\frac{1}{1100}$, and synchron-ised Compur. *Viewfinder:* open frame. *Rangefinder:* coupled. *Special features:* both shutters operated by same body release, the Compur being electrically operated from built-in batteries which also fire flash-bulbs; rise and fall front, upward tilt; triple extension; rack focusing.

V.N. Press. *Size:* 9×12 cm.; plate, etc. *Lenses:* Ross Xpres 6 in., *f.* 4·5; Ross Xpres wide-angle 4 in., *f.* 4; Teleros Telephoto. *Shutter:* focal plane to $\frac{1}{1000}$, synchronised. *Viewfinders:* open frame for standard and wide-angle lenses. *Special features:* no baseboard; quick-change back.

Vaido Technical. *Sizes:* $3\frac{1}{2} \times 2\frac{1}{2}$ in., 5×4 in., and $\frac{1}{2}$-plate; plate. *Lenses:* various, interchangeable. *Shutter:* focal plane, $\frac{1}{8}$ to $\frac{1}{1000}$. *Special features:* folding, with baseboard; rack focusing; double extension; rotating back; rise and fall front; teak.

2

Where photographs have to be taken under non-average conditions, however, additional lenses have to be provided.

Supplementary Lenses. If the standard lens is so mounted on the camera that it it not intended to be moved (and this applies to practically all lenses which have the shutter mechanism in the same mount), variation of standard working can be achieved only by means of supplementary lenses; i.e. lenses which are added to a standard lens and which vary its effective focal length. The supplementary lenses are divided into two categories: positive, which shorten the effective focal length of a standard lens; and negative, which lengthen the effective focal length.

The commonest form of positive supplementary lens is the "portrait attachment," used principally to enable close-ups to be taken with a box-camera lens which, without the attachment, would not focus at less than about 10 ft.

Negative supplementary lenses are somewhat specialist in their applications, and can be used only in those cameras which have double or triple extension facilities or to which extension tubes can be fitted.

Positive Supplementaries. When a positive supplementary is provided for any particular camera as a portrait attachment, data for its use are generally provided with it. Positive supplementaries of a general nature may be obtained, however, their strengths being expressed in "dioptres," the values most readily obtainable being $+1$, $+1\frac{1}{2}$, $+2$, $+2\frac{1}{2}$, $+3$ and $+4$. The effects of using positive supplementaries with standard lenses will be found accompanying the tables on focusing (depth of field) on page 31.

Interchangeable Lenses. In the case of cameras in which the shutter mechanism is separate from the lens mount (i.e. focal-plane shutters or shutters which work in front of or behind the lens assembly), the entire lens may be changed, and this facility is provided in many precision cameras of small negative size. In general, the interchangeable lenses are:

Wide Angle, having shorter focal length and a larger angle of acceptance than the standard lens of the camera; and

Telephoto, having longer focal length and a smaller angle of acceptance than the standard lens.

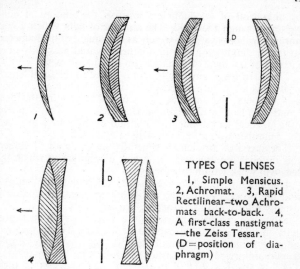

TYPES OF LENSES

I, Simple Mensicus.
2, Achromat. 3, Rapid
Rectilinear—two Achro-
mats back-to-back. 4,
A first-class anastigmat
—the Zeiss Tessar.
(D = position of dia-
phragm)

Wide-angle lenses are used where there is insufficient space
between camera and image to include the whole of the image
with the standard lens. Telephoto lenses are used when it is
desirable to make a picture having a close-up effect from a
greater distance than is possible with a standard lens, and
since lenses having telephoto characteristics can produce
pictures of good perspective and a minimum of foreshortening,
they are often used for making close-up portraits when distance from camera to subject permits.

Lens Speed

The speed at which a picture can be taken is dependent upon
(i) the aperture at which the lens can be used without distortion; (ii) the type of negative emulsion; and (iii) the strength
of the light. The last two factors are dealt with in the section
on Exposure; only the first is considered here.

Accompanying every lens is a diaphragm, a device which,

by alteration of its diameter, controls the amount of light passing through the lens. The amount of light which a diaphragm will pass varies inversely as the square of its diameter, so that a diaphragm of $\frac{1}{2}$ in. diameter would pass only one-quarter of the light of a diaphragm of 1 in. diameter.

The diameter of any diaphragm is linked to the focal length of its lens in definite proportions, the results being described as *f*-numbers. An *f*-number is calculated by dividing the focal length of a lens by its accompanying diameter. Thus if a lens of 2-in. focal length has a diaphragm opening of 1 in., then the *f*-number would be 2—usually written *f*. 2.

The speed of any lens is generally stated as an *f*-number, this number representing the largest diaphragm at which the lens will work without distortion.

Diaphragm *f*-numbers are usually referred to as "stops," and the process of making a diaphragm diameter smaller is usually referred to as "stopping down."

Stops are generally marked on a lens mount in such proportion that (with the exception of the largest) any stop will admit one-half of the light of the next larger. As an example, a medium-priced camera bears the following stop markings: *f*. 4·5, *f*. 5·6, *f*. 8, *f*.11, *f*. 16, *f*. 22, *f*. 32. The first of these markings represents the highest speed of the lens, and comparison of the speeds of the other markings can be obtained from the table which follows.

Equivalent Speeds at Different Stops

In the table opposite, the lens aperture *f*. 8 is given the arbitrary value 1. To find the relative amount of light admitted, and therefore the exposure applicable to any chosen aperture, multiply the exposure time for *f*. 8 by the factor shown.

Some cameras are still marked with U.S. (Uniform System) numbers, and these are shown for convenience. The system is not now in general use.

On certain inexpensive cameras, stops are sometimes marked as 1, 2, 3, 4, or as 1, 2, 3.

When stops are marked as 1, 2, 3, 4, use them as *f*. 11, *f*. 16, *f*. 22 and *f*. 32 respectively. When stops are marked 1, 2, 3, use them as *f*. 11, *f*. 16 and *f*. 22 respectively.

f. No.	U.S. No.	Factor	f. No.	U.S. No.	Factor
1		$\frac{1}{64}$	6·8		$\frac{2}{3}$
1·5		$\frac{1}{32}$	7		$\frac{3}{4}$
1·8		$\frac{1}{30}$	8 (or 7·7)	4	1
1·9		$\frac{1}{20}$	9		$1\frac{1}{4}$
2	0·25	$\frac{1}{16}$	10		$1\frac{1}{2}$
2·5		$\frac{1}{10}$	11 (or 11·3)	8	2
2·8	0·5	$\frac{1}{8}$	12·5		$2\frac{1}{2}$
3·5		$\frac{1}{5}$	14		3
4	1	$\frac{1}{4}$	16	16	4
4·5		$\frac{1}{3}$	22	32	8
5·6	2	$\frac{1}{2}$	32	64	16
6·3		$\frac{5}{8}$	45	128	32

Focal Length

The focal length of any lens is the distance between lens and negative emulsion when the camera is focused upon infinity, and for practical purposes the focal length is directly related to the size of the negative to be made, in the sense that the larger the negative the farther away must be the lens in order to cover the negative area adequately.

The size of any negative is reckoned to be the length of its diagonal, and suitable focal lengths of lenses for different sizes of negatives are shown in the following table:

Negative size (in.)	$1\frac{1}{2} \times 1$	$1\frac{5}{8} \times 2\frac{1}{2}$	$2\frac{1}{4} \times 3\frac{1}{4}$	$3\frac{1}{4} \times 4\frac{1}{4}$	$4\frac{3}{4} \times 6\frac{1}{2}$
Length of negative diagonal (in.) .	$1\frac{3}{4}$	3	4	$5\frac{3}{8}$	$8\frac{1}{8}$
Convenient focal length of lens (in.)	2	3	$4\frac{1}{4}$	$5\frac{1}{2}$	$8\frac{1}{2}$

The focal length of any lens has practical bearing upon two considerations in the matter of focus: (i) hyperfocal distance; and (ii) depth of field. Before dealing with them, it is necessary to note an important point about focus.

It can be said that there is no such thing as perfect focus;

a picture may be said to be in focus if, having regard to the characteristics of the human eye, it looks acceptably sharp at the distance from which it is viewed.

In terms of measurement, the human eye will accept as sharp a point which is about $\frac{1}{100}$ in. across when viewed from a distance of less than 12 in.; therefore a picture which is made up of a number of points of such diameter will be regarded by a viewer as sharply in focus all over. The point just referred to is called in photography a "circle of confusion."

The circle of confusion of $\frac{1}{100}$ in. is the size which would be acceptable on a print; therefore it would only be acceptable in a negative if the print is made from it by contact. If the negative is to be enlarged, then the circle of confusion which is acceptable is in inverse proportion to the number of times of enlargement. A 2 × enlargement would require a negative having a circle of confusion no greater than $\frac{1}{200}$ in. and a 5 × enlargement, $\frac{1}{500}$ in.

This matter of the size of the circle of confusion has a considerable bearing upon focus, for (it having already been stated that there is no such thing as perfect focus) it is necessary to decide how far from perfect focus a picture can be in its various parts and yet still be acceptably sharp. In general it may be said that a circle of confusion greater than $\frac{1}{100}$ in. on the print will result in an out-of-focus effect, and that modern standards aim at a maximum circle of confusion of about $\frac{1}{250}$ in. for viewing at 12 in. or less.

Depth of Field

When a lens is focused at a certain distance, all parts of the image at that distance will be as sharply in focus as the definition of the lens will permit; but as parts of the image are nearer to or further away from the focus-distance so will focus deteriorate gradually until distances are reached where the focus is so bad that the picture can no longer be considered sharp. The two limits—in front of and behind the focus-distance—at which the picture is just acceptably sharp constitute "depth of field."

Bearing in mind the foregoing notes, it may be taken as a rule that the greater the degree of enlargement required for the print, the smaller must be the circle of confusion on the negative, and hence the narrower will be the depth of field—i.e. the smaller will be the distances of acceptable focus in front of and behind the focus-distance of the lens.

It may be noted now that, subject to the degree of unsharpness which will be tolerated in the final print, the circle of confusion is of somewhat arbitrary measurement. A safe rule for general work is to use one-thousandth of the focal length of the lens; thus with a 2-in. lens a circle of confusion of $\frac{1}{500}$ in. would be aimed at.

Apart from these considerations, the extent of the depth of field is also varied by the size of the stop: the smaller the stop, the greater the depth of field, and vice versa.

Hyperfocal Distance

The hyperfocal distance may be described as the distance upon which any lens must be focused to give the greatest depth of field, and depends upon three factors: (i) the focal length of the lens: (ii) the stop at which the lens is to be used; and (iii) the desired circle of confusion. If the hyperfocal distance for any given set of values is known, the working out of depth of focus becomes a matter of the utmost simplicity.

If it is accepted that the circle of confusion is to be one-thousandth of the focal length of a lens, then hyperfocal distance may be worked out from the formula:

$$H = \frac{1000F}{f}$$

where H = hyperfocal distance; F = focal length of lens; and f = f-number of stop at which lens is used.

Once the hyperfocal distance is known, the limits of the depth of field are given by:

$$\frac{HD}{H+D} \quad \text{and} \quad \frac{HD}{H-D}$$

where D = the distance at which the lens is focused. The first formula gives the near limit of the depth of field; the second the far limit.

For example, suppose that a lens of 3-in. focal length is being used at f. 8, and that a photograph is to be taken of an object 20 ft. away. How far in front of and behind that object will the picture be in focus at the standard (in terms of circle of confusion) set?

Using the above formulæ:

$$\text{hyperfocal distance} = \frac{1000 \times 3}{8} = 375 \text{ in.} = 31\tfrac{1}{4} \text{ ft.}$$

and limits of depth of field are:

$$\frac{31 \cdot 25 \times 20}{31 \cdot 25 + 20} = \frac{625}{51 \cdot 25} = 12 \cdot 2 \text{ ft.}$$

and

$$\frac{31 \cdot 25 \times 20}{31 \cdot 25 - 20} = \frac{625}{11 \cdot 25} = 55 \cdot 5 \text{ ft.}$$

Thus everything would be in focus between, say, $12\tfrac{1}{2}$ and 55 ft.

A point to be noted here is that, since focus of the lens is at 20 ft., the nearer point is only $7\tfrac{1}{2}$ ft. in front of that distance, while the farther point is 35 ft. behind it. Herein lies the rule for all focusing: focus is always lost appreciably sooner in those parts of the picture nearer to the camera than the distance focused upon. In practice, if the focus of nearer objects is given care, the focus of farther objects will (within reasonable limits) look after itself.

Where the owner of a camera uses only one lens and decides that he will always use his standard of focus as one-thousandth of the focal length of that lens, he can establish a factor for his lens which will simplify working out hyperfocal distance by simply multiplying the focal length by 1000. The result, divided by the aperture he intends to use for any particular picture, will give him the hyperfocal distance at once.

A table of hyperfocal distances will be found on page 30.

Depth of Field Tables

Based on the table on page 30, the following tables show depth of field for lenses of different focal lengths. In each entry, the first figure gives the nearer limit, the second figure the farther limit. For practical use, the distances (which are in feet and inches) have been slightly evened off.

Each cell shows the near and far limits of sharp focus as feet : inches, written here as `near / far`.

Distance focused	Stop								
	22	16	11	8	5·6	4·5	4	3·5	2
3 ft.	2:1 / 5:0	2:4 / 4:2	2:6 / 3:9	2:7 / 3:6	2:8 / 3:4	2:9 / 3:3	2:9 / 3:3	2:9 / 3:3	2:11 / 3:1
4 ft.	2:8 / 8:7	2:11 / 6:6	3:2 / 5:5	3:4 / 4:11	3:7 / 4:7	3:8 / 4:5	3:8 / 4:5	3:9 / 4:4	3:10 / 4:2
5 ft.	3:0 / 15:0	3:5 / 9:7	3:9 / 7:6	4:1 / 6:7	4:4 / 6:0	4:5 / 5:9	4:6 / 5:8	4:7 / 5:7	4:9 / 5:3
6 ft.	3:4 / 30:0	3:10 / 14:2	4:4 / 9:11	4:8 / 8:5	5:0 / 7:6	5:2 / 7:2	5:3 / 7:0	5:4 / 6:9	5:8 / 6:5
10 ft.	4:4 / ∞	5:2 / ∞	6:0 / 29:0	6:9 / 19:3	7:6 / 15:0	7:11 / 13:8	8:1 / 13:2	8:3 / 12:8	8:11 / 11:4
15 ft.	5:0 / ∞	6:2 / ∞	7:6 / ∞	8:9 / 50:0	10:0 / 30:0	10:8 / 25:0	11:0 / 23:6	11:5 / 22:0	12:8 / 18:3
20 ft.	5:6 / ∞	6:10 / ∞	8:7 / ∞	10:2 / ∞	12:0 / 60:0	13:0 / 43:0	13:6 / 38:0	14:1 / 34:0	16:1 / 26:0
30 ft.	6:0 / ∞	7:9 / ∞	10:0 / ∞	12:4 / ∞	14:11 / ∞	16:7 / 155:0	17:6 / 105:0	18:5 / 55:0	22:1 / 47:0
50 ft.	6:6 / ∞	8:7 / ∞	11:7 / ∞	14:9 / ∞	18:8 / ∞	21:3 / ∞	22:9 / ∞	24:4 / ∞	31:3 / 120:0
Inf.	7:6	10:5	15:1	20:10	29:9	37:1	41:8	47:7	83:6

Depth of Field—3-in. (75–80-mm.) Lens

Stop

Distance focused	22	16	11	8	5·6	4·5	4	3·5	2
3 ft.	2 : 5 / 4 : 4	2 : 7 / 3 : 8	2 : 8 / 3 : 5	2 : 9 / 3 : 3	2 : 10 / 3 : 2	2 : 11 / 3 : 2	2 : 11 / 3 : 1	2 : 11 / 3 : 1	*
4 ft.	3 : 0 / 6 : 2	3 : 3 / 5 : 4	3 : 5 / 4 : 10	3 : 7 / 4 : 7	3 : 8 / 4 : 5	3 : 9 / 4 : 4	3 : 10 / 4 : 3	3 : 10 / 4 : 2	3 : 11 / 4 : 1
5 ft.	3 : 6 / 8 : 10	3 : 10 / 7 : 4	4 : 2 / 6 : 5	4 : 4 / 6 : 0	4 : 6 / 5 : 7	4 : 7 / 5 : 6	4 : 8 / 5 : 5	4 : 8 / 5 : 4	4 : 10 / 5 : 2
6 ft.	3 : 11 / 12 : 8	4 : 4 / 9 : 9	4 : 9 / 8 : 1	5 : 1 / 7 : 5	5 : 4 / 6 : 11	5 : 5 / 6 : 8	5 : 6 / 6 : 7	5 : 7 / 6 : 6	5 : 9 / 6 : 3
10 ft.	5 : 4 / 80 : 0	6 : 2 / 27 : 6	7 : 0 / 17 : 10	7 : 7 / 14 : 8	8 : 2 / 12 : 11	8 : 6 / 12 : 2	8 : 8 / 11 : 10	8 : 10 / 11 : 7	9 : 3 / 10 : 10
15 ft.	6 : 6 / ∞	7 : 8 / ∞	9 : 1 / 44 : 0	10 : 2 / 28 : 9	11 : 3 / 22 : 6	11 : 10 / 20 : 6	12 : 1 / 19 : 8	12 : 5 / 19 : 0	13 : 5 / 17 : 0
25 ft.	7 : 10 / ∞	9 : 8 / ∞	12 : 0 / ∞	14 : 0 / 125 : 0	16 : 0 / 57 : 0	17 : 3 / 54 : 0	17 : 10 / 42 : 0	18 : 6 / 38 : 0	20 : 10 / 31 : 3
50 ft.	9 : 4 / ∞	12 : 0 / ∞	15 : 8 / ∞	19 : 3 / ∞	23 : 8 / ∞	26 : 4 / ∞	27 : 9 / ∞	29 : 5 / 165 : 0	35 : 9 / 83 : 0
Inf.	11 : 5	15 : 8	22 : 9	31 : 3	44 : 6	55 : 6	62 : 6	71 : 3	125 : 0

Depth of Field—4¼-in. (10·5-cm.) Lens

Distance focused					Stop				
	2	3·5	4	4·5	5·6	8	11	16	22
4 ft.	*	3:11 4:2	3:10 4:2	3:10 4:2	3:9 4:3	3:8 4:5	3:7 4:7	3:5 4:11	3:2 5:5
5 ft.	4:11 5:1	4:9 5:3	4:9 5:3	4:9 5:4	4:8 5:5	4:6 5:8	4:4 5:11	4:1 6:7	3:9 7:5
6 ft.	5:10 6:2	5:8 6:5	5:8 6:5	5:6 6:6	5:5 6:8	5:4 7:0	5:1 7:5	4:9 8:4	4:5 9:10
10 ft.	9:6 10:7	9:2 11:0	9:0 11:3	8:10 11:6	8:8 11:9	8:2 13:0	7:8 14:6	7:0 18:6	6:3 28:0
15 ft.	14:0 16:3	13:2 17:6	12:11 18:0	12:7 18:6	12:2 19:6	11:4 22:6	10:6 28:0	9:0 50:0	8:0 ∞
30 ft.	26:6 35:0	24:0 41:0	23:6 44:0	23:0 48:0	21:0 57:0	19:0 100:0	16:6 ∞	13:0 ∞	11:0 ∞
50 ft.	40:0 65:0	36:0 95:0	33:0 115:0	31:6 140:0	30:0 ∞	25:0 ∞	22:0 ∞	16:0 ∞	12:6 ∞
100 ft.	75:0	60:0	50:0	47:0	41:0	32:0	25:0	20:0	15:0

* *Depth of field negligible.*

Depth of Field—5½-in. (13·5-cm.) Lens

Distance focused	Stop 3·5	4·5	5·6	6·3	8	11	16	22	32
5 ft.	4:10 / 5:2	4:10 / 5:3	4:9 / 5:4	4:9 / 5:4	4:8 / 5:5	4:6 / 5:8	4:3 / 6:0	4:0 / 6:7	3:9 / 7:8
4 ft.	5:9 / 6:3	5:8 / 6:4	5:7 / 6:5	5:7 / 6:6	5:6 / 6:8	5:3 / 7:0	5:0 / 7:7	4:8 / 8:5	4:3 / 10:4
8 ft.	7:7 / 8:6	7:5 / 8:8	7:4 / 8:10	7:3 / 8:11	7:0 / 9:3	6:9 / 9:11	6:3 / 11:0	5:10 / 13:0	5:2 / 18:0
10 ft.	9:4 / 10:10	9:2 / 11:1	8:11 / 11:5	8:10 / 11:7	8:6 / 12:0	8:0 / 13:0	7:6 / 15:0	6:9 / 19:0	6:0 / 33:0
15 ft.	13:6 / 17:0	13:1 / 17:6	12:8 / 18:0	12:5 / 19:0	12:0 / 20:0	11:0 / 23:0	9:10 / 31:0	8:9 / 53:0	7:4 / ∞
30 ft.	24:6 / 39:0	23:3 / 42:0	22:0 / 47:0	21:0 / 50:0	19:9 / 63:0	17:6 / 105:0	14:9 / ∞	12:3 / ∞	9:9 / ∞
50 ft.	36:0 / 81:0	33:6 / 98:0	31:0 / 125:0	29:9 / 155:0	26:9 / ∞	22:9 / ∞	18:3 / ∞	14:9 / ∞	11:3 / ∞
100 ft.	60:0	51:0	45:0	42:6	36:6	29:6	22:3	17:3	12:6

Depth of Field—8½-in. (21·5-cm.) Lens

Distance focused	Stop 4·5	5·6	8	11	16	22	32	45
6 ft.	5 : 10 / 6 : 3	5 : 9 / 6 : 4	5 : 8 / 6 : 5	5 : 6 / 6 : 7	5 : 3 / 7 : 0	5 : 1 / 7 : 5	4 : 9 / 8 : 5	4 : 4 / 9 : 8
8 ft.	7 : 8 / 8 : 5	7 : 7 / 8 : 6	7 : 4 / 8 : 9	7 : 1 / 9 : 0	6 : 10 / 9 : 8	6 : 5 / 10 : 7	5 : 8 / 12 : 6	5 : 4 / 16 : 3
10 ft.	9 : 5 / 10 : 8	9 : 3 / 10 : 10	9 : 0 / 11 : 4	8 : 8 / 11 : 9	8 : 3 / 12 : 10	7 : 8 / 14 : 6	6 : 10 / 18 : 3	5 : 11 / 27 : 6
15 ft.	13 : 9 / 16 : 6	13 : 5 / 17 : 0	12 : 10 / 18 : 0	12 : 2 / 19 : 7	11 : 1 / 22 : 8	10 : 3 / 28 : 0	9 : 0 / 46 : 0	7 : 8 / ∞
30 ft.	25 : 3 / 37 : 0	24 : 3 / 39 : 0	22 : 5 / 48 : 0	20 : 5 / 56 : 0	17 : 9 / 92 : 0	15 : 9 / ∞	12 : 8 / ∞	10 : 4 / ∞
50 ft.	38 : 0 / 73 : 0	36 : 0 / 82 : 0	32 : 0 / 115 : 0	28 : 3 / 220 : 0	23 : 0 / ∞	20 : 0 / ∞	15 : 4 / ∞	11 : 10 / ∞
100 ft.	62 : 0 / 270 : 0	55 : 0 / ∞	47 : 0 / ∞	40 : 0 / ∞	31 : 0 / ∞	25 : 0 / ∞	18 : 0 / ∞	13 : 6 / ∞

Hyperfocal Distances Table
(Circle of confusion = one-thousandth of focal length)

Focal length of lens (in.)	Stop								
	2	3·5	4	4·5	5·6	8	11	16	22
2	83·5	47·6	41·7	37·1	29·7	20·9	15·1	10·5	7·5
3	125·0	71·4	62·5	55·6	44·6	31·2	22·7	15·6	11·4
4½	177·1	101·2	88·5	78·7	63·2	44·3	32·2	22·1	16·1
5¼	229·2	131·0	114·6	101·8	81·8	57·3	41·7	28·7	20·9
8½	354·2	202·4	177·1	157·4	126·5	88·5	64·4	44·3	32·2

Distances are in feet to the nearest single place of decimals.

Focusing Distances: Conversion Tables

Feet into metres		Metres into feet	
Feet	Metres	Metres	Feet
3	0·91	1	3·28
4	1·22	2	6·56
5	1·52	3	9·84
6	1·83	4	13·12
7	2·13	5	16·40
8	2·44	6	19·69
9	2·74	7	22·96
10	3·04	8	26·25
12	3·65	9	29·50
15	4·57	10	32·80
18	5·48	11	36·10
20	6·09	12	39·40
25	7·61	13	42·65
30	9·13	14	45·90
35	10·64	15	49·20
40	12·16	16	52·50
45	13·68	17	55·75
50	15·22	18	59·00
60	18·26	19	62·30
70	21·30	20	65·60
80	24·35	25	82·00
90	27·40	30	98·40
100	30·43	35	114·80

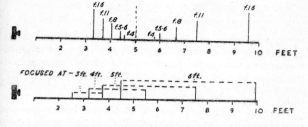

DEPTHS OF FIELD

Top: Depth of field increases as a lens is stopped down—lens in diagram is 2 in. focal length; focus set at 5 ft.; depths of field indicated for *f*-nos. 4, 5·6, 8, 11 and 16

Bottom: Depth of field also increases as focus-distance is increased—focal length 2 in.; stop *f.*11; focus-distances indicated are 3, 4, 5 and 6 ft.

Positive Supplementary Lenses

In the table below, the distances given are those from camera lens to subject, and are applicable only to cameras which have a focusing scale and with focus set at infinity.

Box cameras which, without a supplementary lens, will focus from about 10 ft. to infinity, are not necessarily set for infinity focus, but probably at about 25 ft. for lens of 3-in. focal length, and at about 20 ft. for lens of 4¼-in. focal length. In such cases "portrait attachments" should be obtained from the makers of the cameras concerned, and the tables issued with such attachments consulted.

Power of sup. lens (in dioptres)	Sharpest focus (lens-to-subject) at (in.)
+1	39·4
+1½	26·25
+2	19·7
+2½	15·75
+3	13·1
+4	9·85

SHUTTERS

THE TWO types of shutter used in practically all general photography are the focal-plane and the diaphragm between-lens. As a general rule, the focal-plane shutter permits the facility of interchangeable lenses; the diaphragm between-lens shutter does not, unless the entire shutter mechanism is to be changed with the lens.

There are two other types; the diaphragm behind-lens and the before-lens of many patterns. Both of these types permit lens changes.

Focal-plane

This type of shutter is placed as close as possible to the surface of the negative material, and is made of metal, plastic or other suitable material. Length of exposure is varied in two ways: by altering the speed at which a slit in the shutter passes across the negative material, and by altering the size of the slit. The type can be synchronised for flash, and can be fitted with delayed-action mechanism and devices for automatic setting and for the prevention of double exposures, the setting of the shutter (in the case of film cameras) winding on the film for the next exposure.

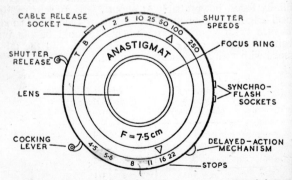

TYPICAL SHUTTER ASSEMBLY for a 7·5 cm. (3 in.) lens, with 8 speeds plus T and B, and other principal features

Between-lens

This type is positioned between the elements of multiple anastigmat lenses, and close to that other (iris) diaphragm which regulates the size of the stop opening. It may be self-cocking (i.e. operated by the movement of the shutter release lever) or may have to be set before release by the operation of a separate lever. It may be fitted with all the devices named for the focal-plane type.

Simple Shutters

In the case of box cameras which have single (meniscus or achromat) lenses, the usual rule is to fit a simple self-cocking shutter which is no more than a plate with a hole in it, the hole passing before or behind the lens at a predetermined speed when making the exposure. Such shutters are frequently synchronised for flash (foil or wire-filled bulbs of the long-flash type), but do not have other devices.

Shutter Speeds

Simple shutters are generally set for a single ("instantaneous") speed of about $\frac{1}{25}$ or $\frac{1}{30}$ sec., and for either T (=Time) or B (=Bulb) exposures.

(With T settings, the shutter release is operated to open the shutter, and operated again separately to close the shutter. With B settings, the shutter release is pressed to open the shutter, held for so long as the shutter is to remain open, and then released to permit the shutter to close.)

Multiple-speed shutters are usually of two kinds: fast speeds only, and fast and slow speeds. The first kind generally operates from $\frac{1}{25}$ sec.; the second from 1 or $\frac{1}{2}$ sec. Usual speeds found in shutters are: 1, $\frac{1}{2}$, $\frac{1}{5}$, $\frac{1}{10}$, $\frac{1}{25}$, $\frac{1}{50}$, $\frac{1}{100}$, $\frac{1}{150}$, $\frac{1}{200}$, $\frac{1}{250}$, $\frac{1}{300}$, $\frac{1}{500}$ and (focal-plane only) $\frac{1}{1000}$. Not all of these speeds will be found on every shutter, and there are some variations from the above values.

The following table shows some of the characteristics of selected between-lens shutters.

Some of these shutters are fitted with delayed-action mechanism; inquiries should be made at the time of purchase. Where shutters are not synchronised for flash, contacts can be fitted by skilled mechanics.

3

Between-lens Shutter List

Name	No. of speeds	Range of speeds	Flash Synchronisation
Agilux 4 . .	4	$\frac{1}{25}$ to $\frac{1}{125}$, B	Wire and Foil Bulbs
Agilux 8 . .	8	1 to $\frac{1}{150}$, B	Wire and Foil Bulbs
Compur . .	8	1 to $\frac{1}{250}$, B, T	
Compur-Rapid X .	9	1 to $\frac{1}{500}$, B	Wire, Foil, SM (at slower speeds), Electronic
Compur-Rapid MX	9	1 to $\frac{1}{500}$, B	All bulbs, all speeds
Epsilon 4 . .	4	$\frac{1}{25}$ to $\frac{1}{250}$, B, T	Wire, Foil and SM at slower speeds
Epsilon 8 . .	8	1 to $\frac{1}{250}$, B, T	Wire, Foil and SM at slower speeds
Klio . . .	8	1 to $\frac{1}{175}$, B, T	
Pronto . . .	4	$\frac{1}{25}$ to $\frac{1}{200}$, B	Wire, Foil and SM at slower speeds
Prontor S . .	8	1 to $\frac{1}{300}$, B	Wire, Foil at slower speeds; SM at all speeds
Prontor SV . .	8	1 to $\frac{1}{300}$, B	All bulbs, all speeds

Details of the firing speeds of flash bulbs will be found o
page 65.

FILTERS

Colour Response of Negative Materials

All negative materials "see" colours differently from th
human eye, with the result that, in terms of black-and-whit
the resultant luminosities in a print are not the same as th
impression of those luminosities recorded by the eye dire
from the image. The best and commonest example of th
is to be seen in the eye-impression and the print-impressio
of a blue sky with white clouds. To the eye, the blue of th
sky seems much darker than the white of the clouds; yet o
the print both of these colours appear at about the same i
tensity in terms of black-and-white. (For differences of colou
renderings in colour material see the section on Colou
Photography).

The exact response of negative material to colours depends upon the type of negative material used, the results as seen on the print being:

Negative material	Colour response			
	Blue	Green	Yellow	Red
Ordinary . .	Too much	Too little	Too little	None
Orthochromatic .	Too much	Correct	Too little	None
Panchromatic	Too much	Too little	Correct	Too much
Panchromatic*	Too much	Correct	Correct	Correct

It will be noted from the above that all kinds of negative material are too sensitive to blue, and respond to the other colours in various ways. Thus ordinary negative material

MATERIAL	BLUE	GREEN	YELLOW	RED

NEGATIVE SENSITIVITY TO COLOUR

In this chart, materials are given arbitrary values of 3 (highest sensitivity) to 0.

Note that all materials are over-sensitive to blue

will give prints in which the blues are white, the greens and yellows are too dark, and the reds are black.

Examples of the various types of negative material as classified above are:

Ordinary. Process materials (not used for general photography); and some materials marked Standard or Regular.

Orthochromatic. The "chromes" generally (Verichrome, Selochrome, Plenachrome, Sensichrome, Superchrome, etc.), and material marked Ortho (Ortho Portrait, Commercial Ortho, Ortho Press, etc.).

Panchromatic*. In general, the high-speed panchromatic materials (Super Press, HP3, P.1500, Ultrapan, etc.).

Panchromatic. In general, lower-speed, fine-grain panchromatic materials (Isopan FF, Finopan, FP Special, Microgran, Panatomic X, Plus X, etc.).

Colour Correction

To correct to some extent the colour effects as they will be seen in the final print, it is necessary to modify the colour of the light passing through the camera lens, and this is done by means of filters—disks of coloured material (glass or gelatine) —placed in front of or within or behind the lens mount.

The effect of a filter must be to hold back that part of the light to which a negative material is too sensitive, and to admit relatively more of that part of the light to which a negative material is not sensitive enough. In practice, any filter will pass any light of or near to its own colour, and will tend to stop any light opposite to its own colour. Thus:

Filter of colour		Will pass	Will stop
Blue .	.	Blue	Yellow
Yellow	.	Yellow	Blue
Green	.	Green	Red
Red .	.	Red	Green

The amount of any colour which will be passed or stopped by any filter is not absolute, but is graduated according to the depth of the colour of the filter. Thus a very deep yellow will stop nearly all blue, but a light-yellow filter will stop only a part of blue.

Adjustment of Exposure

Since the very purpose of a filter is to stop some of the light reaching negative material, it follows that, when using a filter, some increase of exposure must be given in order that the negative material shall not be under-exposed.

A point to be noted is that, while most negative materials have considerable latitude in the matter of exposure errors, it is necessary to disregard that latitude to a great extent when using a filter, for under-exposure will exaggerate the effect of a filter, while over-exposure will largely cancel out any correction a filter was meant to apply.

The amount of increase of exposure for any filter depends upon the colour and strength of the filter and the type of negative material being used. Exposure factors, together with a guide to the use of filters, are given in the tables below. (It should be noted that filters have a slightly smaller factor for panchromatic materials than for ortho.)

Correction Filters

For Ortho

Subject	No filter	Filter and exp. factor	Results
Blue sky .	Nearly white	Light yellow (×2) Med. yellow (×2½) Deep yellow (×4)	Improvement Correct Too dark
Landscape .	Distance hazy	Med. yellow (×2½)	Reduced haze
Sunset . (blue sky)	Little contrast	Med. yellow (×2½) Deep yellow (×4)	Good contrast Dramatic
Portraits .	Lips dark	Light yellow (×2) Med. yellow (×2½)	Improvement Correct

Notes on Correction Filters for Ortho

1. Filters of colours other than those given above are not recommended for use with ortho.

2. Portraits on ortho by artificial light are nearly correct; a light-yellow filter ($\times 1\frac{1}{2}$ by half-watt or photoflood) will in many cases give improvement.

For Pan

Subject	No filter	Filter and exp. factor	Result
Blue sky .	Too light	Light yellow ($\times 1\frac{1}{2}$) Med. yellow ($\times 2$) Deep yellow ($\times 3$) Orange ($\times 5$) Med. red ($\times 7$)	Correct Slightly dark Fairly dark Dramatic Nearly black
Landscape .	Distance hazy	Med. Yellow ($\times 2$) Orange ($\times 5$)	Reduction of haze Almost clear
Sunset . . (blue sky)	Contrast good	Med. yellow ($\times 2$) Deep yellow ($\times 3$) Med. red ($\times 7$)	Improvement Correct Dramatic
Portraits (by daylight)	Good result	Light yellow ($\times 1\frac{1}{2}$) Med. yellow ($\times 2$)	Correct Improved sky background
Portraits . (by art. light)	Blue eyes too light; lips too dark (on Pan.)	Light blue ($\times 1\frac{1}{2}$)	Correct

For the photographer who wishes to carry only one general purpose filter, the most useful colour is medium yellow (for ortho, $\times 2\frac{1}{2}$ in daylight and $\times 2$ in artificial light; for pan $\times 2$ in daylight and $\times 1\frac{1}{2}$ in artificial light).

The next most useful are probably orange (pan, $\times 5$) for penetration of haze, and light blue (pan, $\times 1\frac{1}{2}$) for portraiture by artificial light.

Effect Filters

Apart from correction, filters are used to achieve special effects by lightening or darkening certain colours in the print. As a simple example, if it is desired to photograph a green car standing close to a red brick wall, and the effect is to be that of a light-coloured car against a dark background, a green filter (passing green, stopping red) would be used.

In selecting a filter for effect, the following table will be of assistance:

Colour of filter	Tends to lighten	Tends to darken
Yellow . .	Yellow-orange, orange; yellow-green, green	Violet, red-violet, blue-violet, blue and blue-green
Orange . .	Yellow, yellow-orange; red-orange, red	Violet, blue-violet, blue, blue-green, and green
Red . .	Orange, orange-red; red-violet, violet	Yellow, yellow-green, green, blue and blue-green
Violet . .	Red, red-violet; blue, blue-violet	Orange, yellow-orange, yellow, green and yellow-green
Blue . .	Violet, blue-violet; green, blue-green	Orange, orange-red, red-yellow and yellow-orange
Green . .	Yellow, yellow-green; blue, blue-green	Red, orange, orange-red, violet and red-violet

Notes:

A colour which is the same colour as the filter will be passed as almost white.

Filters used for effect should have applied to them the exposure factors advised by the makers.

Infra-red Photography

Specialised negative material is available which is sensitive to blue and to red and infra-red, and which is not sensitive to other colours. This material, when used with a strong red filter which eliminates blue, is particularly useful for:

1. Making pictures of distant landscapes which are practically or wholly obscured by haze;

2. Making pictures in daylight which will have all the effects of having been made at night; and

3. Taking pictures by the so-called "black light" (i.e. infra-red rays which are not visible to the eye).

Infra-red photography calls for long exposures mostly, although flash-bulbs are made which are dyed for infra-red emission with small visible radiation and which enable shutter speeds as short as $\frac{1}{50}$ sec. to be used.

Polarisers

Strictly, a polariser is not a filter but a screen which is used in front of the lens of a camera for the purpose of cutting off polarised light such as is reflected from highly glazed surfaces (windows, pottery, etc.) and from the clear sky.

Its principal use is for the cutting of reflections, so that objects behind the glass of a window can be photographed without being degraded by reflections of objects in front of the window. But since a polariser will also cut polarised light from a blue sky, it may also be used to achieve effects similar to those given by a yellow filter.

In use, the polariser is held to the eye and revolved until it is seen that the effect required is achieved; the angle to which the polariser has been revolved is then noted, and the polariser is placed over the camera lens at exactly the same angle.

Since a polariser reduces some of the light which can pass through a camera lens, some increase of exposure is necessary when using it. The directions of the makers should be followed in this respect; a usual exposure factor is ×2.

VIEWFINDERS AND RANGEFINDERS

THE TWO principal types of viewfinders are: (i) direct, also referred to as "eye-level"; and (ii) indirect, also referred to as "waist-level."

Direct viewfinders include open-frame and direct vision optical. Focusing screen can, for convenience, be regarded as a direct viewfinder.

Indirect viewfinders include the brilliant and the reflex.

Direct Viewfinders

Open Frame. This viewfinder consists essentially of a wire frame having the proportions of the picture covered by the camera lens, and mounted roughly in the plane of the lens, either above or to one side; and a small eyepiece of peep-sight character mounted at the back of the camera body and lined up with the centre-line of the wire frame. It is used at eye-level.

Direct-vision Optical is also used at eye-level, and consists essentially of the same parts as the open frame, except that frame and eyepiece are mounted close together on the camera body, that the frame is very much smaller, and that both frame and eyepiece are fitted with simple lenses.

Into the direct-vision optical class may be included the viewfinder which is part of and incorporated into a range-finder. It is used in the same way as the direct-vision optical.

Focusing Screen. This method is usual in plate cameras where the plate-holder can be removed from the back and a ground-glass screen substituted. The image to be photo-graphed can be seen projected by the camera lens on to the ground glass (it is a reversed projection—upside down and left-to-right), and by studying the ground-glass the picture can be composed and brought into focus by change of camera position and operation of the focusing control.

Indirect Viewfinders

Brilliant. In this viewfinder, the image is projected by a finder lens on to a mirror set at an angle of 45° to it, and reflected on to a ground-glass or a second lens for viewing from above. The brilliant finder is thus of the reflex type, but is never coupled to the taking lens of the camera for focus. It generally gives a very small image of the picture to be taken, but some cameras incorporate large brilliant finders in which the image is the same size or nearly the same size as the negative area. Brilliant finders are generally fitted to cheaper cameras.

Reflex. This viewfinder works on the same principle as the brilliant, except that the term is reserved invariably for the type which is either coupled to the taking lens of the camera for focus, or actually uses the taking lens. In the first case (a twin-lens reflex camera), the finder has a separate lens of the same focal length as the taking lens, and the two lenses operate together by means of gearing when the focus control is used. In the second case (a single-lens reflex camera), the image is projected by the actual taking lens on to a mirror set at an angle of 45° within the camera body, and so on to a viewing screen. When the shutter release is pressed, the internal mirror automatically swings upwards a fraction of a second in advance of the movement of the shutter. In operation, the twin-lens reflex permits the picture to be viewed at and beyond the time of exposure; with the single-lens reflex the picture disappears from the viewfinder screen immediately before exposure.

Rangefinders

All rangefinders used at the present time work on the same principle, the only differences being in the appearance of the image when looking through the eyepiece.

Basically the rangefinder consists of an eyepiece, a prism and a mirror. The mirror can be turned slightly on its axis by means of a knob which operates over a scale marked in metres or feet, according to design. The accompanying diagram illustrates the arrangement of these elements and the way in which the rangefinder works.

A rangefinder may be used apart from or on the camera but not coupled to the lens, in which case the distance is first found by rangefinder and the camera lens than set for focus; or the rangefinder may be coupled to the lens, in which case setting the rangefinder will automatically set the lens for focus. In operation, the picture to be photographed is viewed through the rangefinder eyepiece, when (if the picture is out of focus) the image will be seen to be split in some way, one part of it not coinciding with the other. The turning of the knob will bring the parts of the image together exactly, and

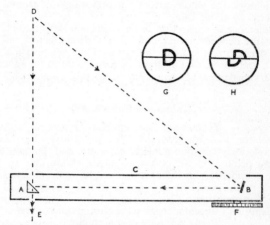

PRINCIPLE OF RANGEFINDER

A prism, A, passes vision from the subject D and from the swivelling mirror B (which is geared to the operating wheel F), giving two images at E. When the images appear as one (G, as distinct from H, for example), the rangefinder is adjusted for correct distance. C = rangefinder casing

the mark on the knob which traverses the distance scale will indicate the distance off. There is no need to read this distance if the rangefinder is coupled to the lens.

It should be noted that some types of coupled rangefinder also act as direct-vision optical viewfinders; others, however, do not, and viewing then must be done as a separate operation after the distance off is found and focus set.

Rangefinders generally will measure accurately from 2 or 3 ft. (or, if marked in metres, from 0·6 or 1 m.) to infinity. Most are fitted with standard accessory shoes.

EXPOSURE AIDS

IN THIS section are included meters proper, tables and calculators, the whole covering a price-range of from a few shillings to about £40.

Reference to the section on Exposure will show that correct exposure depends upon a number of separate factors, such as the strength of the light, the speed of the negative material used, and so on, and all these factors are taken into account in varying degrees of accuracy in meters, tables and calculators.

Tables and Calculators

Exposure Tables are the simplest form of exposure calculator, and are generally self-explanatory. They afford a moderately accurate guide to exposure, and the ones to be found printed on the endpapers of this book may be used with confidence. By their very nature, however, tables cannot cover with precision the whole of the many conditions affecting exposure.

Exposure Calculators enable the photographer to take more of these conditions precisely into account; but they, like the table, are inaccurate to the extent that they call upon the photographer to exercise his own judgment as to the strength of the light, both direct and that reflected from the subject. Nevertheless they will, competently used, give more consistent results than tables. In design they generally have one or more rotating disks pivoted over a scale. The disk or disks are set for the exposure conditions prevailing, and the exposure is then read off. Calculators are of many patterns, but are inexpensive and simple to operate. Full directions are given with each calculator.

Meters

A broad difference between calculator and meter is that a calculator does not measure the strength of light (either direct or reflected), while a meter does. There are four current types of exposure meter: sensitive-paper, extinction, photoelectric and photometer.

Sensitive-paper Meter. In this type, a small strip of sensitive paper is placed next to a tinted strip, and the time taken for the sensitive paper to darken to the colour of the tinted strip is measured by the operator, and the result transferred to a dial, whence the exposure may be read off. The meter is very little more expensive than a calculator.

Extinction Meter. This type is fitted with an eyepiece through which can be seen both the image to be photographed and some figures of varying shades from light to dark. When the image is inspected through the eyepiece, the number which is just visible is noted, and its value transferred to a scale from which exposure may be read. In some meters of this type the figures are replaced by a pattern, half of which may be darkened until it just disappears, the exposure then being read off from knob and dial. This type is rather more expensive than the sensitive-paper meter.

Photo-electric Meter. This type is the one most generally used by serious photographers. It is fairly expensive, but very accurate when used with care. In the main it consists of a photo-electric cell which, when light falls upon it, generates a minute current of electricity, the strength of the current being proportional to the strength of the light. This current is fed to a measuring meter which has a pointer moving over a dial to indicate exposure.

Photometer. This type consists of a tube fitted with an eyepiece at one end, a spot set in the middle of a viewing glass at the other, and a lamp and battery. In use, the spot is illuminated by the lamp, and the image to be photographed is viewed through the eyepiece. The strength of the lamp is then adjusted until both image and spot exactly match each other in terms of brightness. The mechanism by which the strength of the lamp is varied operates over a scale, from which exposure can be read. This type of meter is the most expensive.

General Notes

Meters are scaled and otherwise made for two kinds of light: incident (i.e. direct) or reflected. Most meters are for reflected light, which is to say that they measure the actual light reflected from the image to be photographed, and are pointed towards that part of the image in which most detail is required. Sensitive-paper meters and photo-electric meters have a fairly wide angle of acceptance, and for readings to be accurate they must be held close to that part of the image in which most detail is required, taking care that the image is not shadowed by either the meter or the operator. Extinction meters and photometers, being of direct-vision characteristics, may be pointed from a reasonable distance exactly at the part of the image in which detail is required.

All tables, calculators and meters have variations in style of marking, the variations mostly being for different ways of stating the speeds of negative material (e.g. British Standard, European Scheiner, and so on) more details of which will be found in the section upon Exposure. The markings to be chosen, which will to some extent determine the make of meter, should be those with which the operator is most familiar.

Where a camera does not have a rangefinder, etc., incorporated, it may be fitted with an "accessory shoe," on to which various accessories, fitted with the counterpart of the accessory shoe, may be secured. Many cameras are fitted with an accessory shoe at the time of manufacture.

MISCELLANEOUS ACCESSORIES

For Long Exposures

IT IS generally accepted that few people are steady enough to give an exposure of $\frac{1}{10}$ sec. or longer without evidence of camera shake being seen on negative and print; certainly the results of camera shake will be seen on B and T exposures if the camera is held in the hand. Two pieces of apparatus are necessary for steadiness during long exposures: a means of fixing the camera securely in position, and a means of avoiding camera shake when actually operating the shutter release.

Tripods and Clamps are used for the first purpose. Tripods are three-legged stands with some means of screwing cameras to the top. Outdoor types are made to fold or telescope into small compass for carrying, and will extend to 4 or 5 ft. in height according to the preference of the photographer and the make. No tripod should be accepted which is not perfectly rigid when opened out.

For indoor use, the table tripod—height about 10 in.—is much used. It is generally fitted with rubber-tipped feet so that it will stand firmly on furniture without causing damage.

For both indoor and outdoor use, the clamp is a useful device which can be carried in the pocket. Like the tripod, it has a means of securing the camera; the clamping part has a spring jaw or a screwing device by which it can be fixed to gates, posts, fences, chairs, etc.

A necessary addition to any tripod or clamp is a ball-and-socket head. This head is secured to the top of the tripod or clamp, and the camera is then fixed to it. In use, it enables the camera to be tilted or swung to almost any practicable position and held firmly for exposure.

The Cable Release is essential if the camera is to be kept steady during the actual operation of the shutter release. It screws into a socket in the shutter mount, and release is effected by pressing a knob, the cable being slack at the time. It is better to have a cable release too long rather than too short; 6 in. is a good average size.

Automatic Release. This device is useful when the shutter is not fitted with delay-action mechanism, necessary if the photographer wishes to include himself in any picture. It fits over the knob of the cable release, and is usually set to release the shutter 10–15 sec. after being operated.

Lens Hoods

Since flare is almost inevitable if direct light from the sun or from a source of artificial light falls upon the camera lens, it is necessary in such circumstances to fit a *Lens Hood* over the lens mount. Many photographers use a lens hood always, on the ground that it cuts down stray light falling across the lens surface, resulting in more definite tone separation in the negative and a brighter print.

Lens Coating

For much the same reason many cameras have *Coated Lenses* as standard equipment, and many photographers have their lenses coated when coating has not already been done by the manufacturers. The purpose of coating is to reduce considerably the scattering and reflection of light at air-glass surfaces of lenses, thereby giving greater brilliance to a picture and almost eliminating the risk of lens flare. The coating is usually of magnesium flouride some four-millionths of an inch thick, and a coated lens has a purple coloration when viewed by reflected light. This coloration has absolutely no effect upon colour-rendering on the negative, either black-and-white or colour.

Coated lenses are also referred to as "bloomed" lenses.

Part Two

EXPOSURE

EXPOSURE FACTORS

General Notes on Exposure

WHEN exposing negative material within the camera, the following two basic factors have to be taken into account:
1. The sensitivity to light of the negative material being used; and
2. The strength of the light which reaches the surface of the negative material as a result of the operation of the camera.

Data relating to the first of these factors is almost invariably supplied by the manufacturers of the negative material, and tables for the interpretation of that data are given later.

The second factor is rather less easily arrived at, and calls for a computation based upon the following variables:
  (i) The actinic value of the light falling upon the subject;
  (ii) The actinic value of the light reflected by the subject;
  (iii) The type of development of the negative material to be used;
  (iv) The factor of any filter used on the camera lens; and
  (v) The lens aperture the photographer intends to use.

Each of these considerations, estimated or measured in various ways by the photographer, and set in combination as a single factor against the sensitivity to light of the negative material being used (factor 1 above), will give:
  (vi) The speed of the shutter which is required for correct exposure.

It should be noted that, in the general run of photography many of these considerations are telescoped into simple rule-of-thumb workings. For example, in the cheaper types of cameras which have fixed aperture and fixed shutter-speed it is usual to use a moderate speed of film for summer and a fast film for winter, to pick on bright days for taking pictures and to depend upon the exposure latitude of the film to get good results. Only on rare occasions, in this case, will exposure be strictly correct, but acceptable prints can be obtained by matching mis-exposed negatives to suitable grades of printing paper.

Again, if a fairly versatile camera is used, and an exposure meter is available, the meter will give a fairly accurate measurement of (i) and/or (ii) above; it will also, by presetting on its dial, take into account factor 1 and considerations (iii) and (iv), and its readings will give at a glance (v) and (vi). For example, when a camera has been loaded with a selected negative material of ultra-fine-grain type which is to be developed in an ultra-fine-grain developer, and a filter of $\times 2$ factor is to be used in taking a picture, the meter can be preset for the sensitivity of the negative material, the setting then being modified so that it will indicate about double exposure for fine-grain development and double exposure again for the filter. Its reading, when the light from the subject is measured, will then give aperture and shutter-speed immediately.

Focus

The factors enumerated above will not, of course, result in a sharp picture. Sharpness is a matter for focus, which in turn depends upon the focal length of the lens and the distance of the lens from subject and negative material, and calls for a separate operation.

Correct focus is generally included in any section on exposure because, as an operation, it must be provided just before exposure is made. Nevertheless, the determination of the value of light and the speed of negative material has no bearing whatsoever upon focus.

Data concerning correct focus will be found in the section upon Lenses.

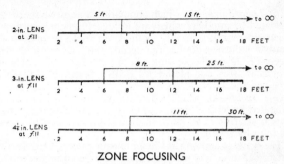

ZONE FOCUSING

Lenses stopped to f.11 and of focal lengths shown may be set for fixed focus-distances for snapshots, and will be in focus over the depths of field indicated. Example: 2-in. lens at 5 ft.; 3 ft. 10 in. to 7 ft. 9 in.; at 15 ft.: 7 ft. 9 in. to infinity.

British Standards

Efforts are being made to standardise exposure considerations, and the British Standards Institution (28 Victoria Street, London, S.W.1) has published various data to that end, in particular in their publication B.S. No. 935: *Photographic Exposure Tables*.

Despite these efforts, manufacturers of negative materials and of exposure meters and calculators are likely to adhere to their own differing systems for many years to come, and for that reason the British Standards, while being mentioned, are not given any special prominence in this book.

NEGATIVE MATERIALS

Indications of Sensitivity

THERE are a number of methods by which the sensitivity to light of negative material is indicated, and these methods fall into three categories:

(i) *Arithmetical*—in which comparative negative speeds are indicated by numbers which are in arithmetical proportion to speed. These indications are H & D, Burroughs Wellcome, General Electric, and Weston.

(ii) *Logarithmic*—in which comparative negative speeds are indicated by numbers which are in logarithmic proportion to speed (in practice, in this method, an increase of 3 in the number indicates double the speed; thus 32° is double the speed of 29°). These indications are European Scheiner (which is also considered as British Scheiner), American Scheiner and DIN.

(iii) *Group*—in which comparative negative speeds are indicated by letters from A to G, group A being the slowest. This indication is to be found on negative materials manufactured by Ilford.

The ways of arriving at these indications vary considerably, but for all practical purposes they may be compared closely by reference to the following table:

Material Speeds Compared

H & D	B.W.	G.E.	West.	Eur. Sch.	Am. Sch.	DIN	B. S. Log	Group
100		3	2	16°	11°	$\frac{5}{10}°$	15°	
125	$\frac{1}{2}$	4	2·5	17°	12°	$\frac{6}{10}°$	16°	A
160	$\frac{1}{3}$	5	3	18°	13°	$\frac{7}{10}°$	17°	
200	$\frac{1}{4}$	6	4	19°	14°	$\frac{8}{10}°$	18°	
250		8	5	20°	15°	$\frac{9}{10}°$	19°	B
320	$\frac{1}{6}$	10	6	21°	16°	$\frac{10}{10}°$	20°	
400		12	8	22°	17°	$\frac{11}{10}°$	21°	
500	$\frac{1}{8}$	16	10	23°	18°	$\frac{12}{10}°$	22°	C
640	$\frac{1}{12}$	20	12	24°	19°	$\frac{13}{10}°$	23°	
800		24	16	25°	20°	$\frac{14}{10}°$	24°	
1000	$\frac{1}{16}$	32	20	26°	21°	$\frac{15}{10}°$	25°	D
1300	$\frac{1}{24}$	40	24	27°	22°	$\frac{16}{10}°$	26°	
1600		50	32	28°	23°	$\frac{17}{10}°$	27°	
2000	$\frac{1}{32}$	64	40	29°	24°	$\frac{18}{10}°$	28°	E
2500	$\frac{1}{48}$	80	50	30°	25°	$\frac{19}{10}°$	29°	
3200		100	64	31°	26°	$\frac{20}{10}°$	30°	
4000	$\frac{1}{64}$	125	80	32°	27°	$\frac{21}{10}°$	31°	F
5000	$\frac{1}{96}$	160	100	33°	28°	$\frac{22}{10}°$	32°	
6400		200	125	34°	29°	$\frac{23}{10}°$	33°	
8000	$\frac{1}{128}$	250	160	35°	30°	$\frac{24}{10}°$	34°	G

Notes:

B.W. numbers are always shown as fractions with the numerator as unity; DIN numbers are always shown as fractions with the denominator as 10.

All numbers in logarithmic indications have the degree sign (°) after them.

G.E. and West. indications refer principally to exposure meter readings. The older versions of the Avo exposure meter are marked in H & D.

Most of the popular negative material available in Britain is marked with a European Scheiner number or a Group letter. Some negative material of European origin is marked in DIN numbers.

Negative Materials List

The following table of some of the more commonly used negative material shows speeds in European Scheiner for both daylight (D) and artificial light (A).

Abbreviations: CF = Cut film; O = Orthochromatic; P = Panchromatic; Pl. = Plates; RF = Roll film; 35 = 35 mm.

Maker	Name of material	Type	Form	Eur. Sch.	
				D	A
Agfa .	Isochrom F	O	35, RF	28°	23°
	Isopan F	P	35, RF	27°	24°
	Isopan FF	P	35, RF	22°	19°
	Isopan ISS	P*	35, RF	32°	30°
Barnet .	FG Pan	P	Pl.	21°	18°
	Presstopan	P*	Pl.	32°	30°
	Sensichrome	O	Pl.	29°	24°
	SS Ortho	O	CF	26°	21°
	Super Press	P*	Pl.	29°	27°
	Ultrapan	P*	CF	32°	30°
Dufay .	Ortho	O	RF	26°	21°
	Pan	P	RF	27°	24°
Ferrania	P3	P	35	27°	24°
	S2	P*	35	32°	30°

Negative Materials List (continued)

Maker	Name of material	Type	Form	Eur. Sch. D	Eur. Sch. A
Ferrania	Super Panchro	P*	RF	32°	30°
	Ultrachromatica	O	RF	29°	24°
Gevaert	Microgran	P	35, RF, CF	27°	24°
	Microgran	P	Pl.	30°	27°
	Panchromosa	P*	All	32°	30°
	Superchrom	O	35, RF, CF	30°	25°
	Superchrom	O	Pl.	32°	27°
Ilford .	Commercial Ortho	O	CF	27°	22°
	FP3	P*	35, RF, CF	29°	27°
	FP Special	P	Pl.	27°	25°
	HP3	P*	35, RF, CF	32°	30°
	HP3	P*	Pl.	34°	32°
	Iso Zenith	O	Pl.	25°	20°
	Press Ortho	O	Pl.	31°	26°
	Selochrome	O	RF, CF, Pl.	29°	24°
	SG Pan	P	Pl.	29°	26°
	SR Pan	P	Pl.	25°	22°
Kodak .	Commercial Ortho	O	CF	26°	21°
	O.250	O	Pl.	19°	14°
	O.800	O	Pl.	30°	25°
	Ortho X	O	CF	34°	29°
	P.300	P*	Pl.	26°	24°
	P.1200	P*	Pl.	32°	30°
	P.1500	P*	Pl.	33°	31°
	Panatomic X	P	35, RF, CF	27°	24°
	Plus X	P	35, RF, CF	29°	26°
	Super XX	P	35, RF, CF	32°	30°
	Verichrome	O	RF	29°	24°

*These panchromatic materials have greater sensitivity to red than the others, and need a blue filter on the lens when taking portraits by artificial light.

The speeds given are effective for normal development; for variations, refer to "Difficult Lighting Conditions" on page 75.

Exposure Latitude

Exposure latitude is the margin of departure from correct exposure which is permissible without seriously affecting the final print.

It is the general rule that negative material will not stand much under-exposure but is tolerant to over-exposure to a rather larger extent. Hence it is better to over-expose than under-expose when in doubt.

Fine-grain materials of slow speed do not have much latitude, and efforts should be made when using such material to determine correct exposure; under-exposure will give somewhat thin results, and considerable over-exposure will to some extent affect the fineness of the grain. Materials of higher speed (especially films of 27° Scheiner and upwards) have greater latitude, and some liberties in the direction of over-exposure (up to, say, 6 or 8 times) may be taken.

Exposure for Fine-grain Development

It should be noted that where any negative material is to be processed in a fine-grain developer, some increase in exposure is necessary in order to achieve good printable contrast with the very gentle reducing agents used in the developer.

Where a developer is purchased ready-compounded, the directions of the maker should be followed strictly. For home-compounded developers, the following increases in exposure apply:

Semi-fine grain	.	No increase
Fine grain	.	$\times 1\frac{1}{2}$ to $\times 2$
Ultra-fine grain	.	$\times 2\frac{1}{2}$ to $\times 4$

Super-sensitising

The speeds of negative materials given in the table immediately above are those applicable to all normal work. On occasions where special exposure circumstances arise, resulting in insufficient light for photography at fast shutter-speeds, the speed of any negative material may be increased by the method described below. The method does not affect fineness of grain.

Obtain a container—a preserving jar, for example—with a completely airtight lid, and into it place 2 or 3 blobs of mercury about the size of split peas. Then place into the container the negative material in its wrappings (the material must not touch the mercury in any way), secure the lid, and leave for 4 days. At the end of that time, use the material in the ordinary way, treating it as having a speed of about twice that stated by the makers. If the material is not used within about a week of treatment, it may be returned to the container for a further 4 days.

Material which, after treatment and exposure, is considered to be somewhat under-exposed may again be placed in the container and left for 3 or 4 days, when under-exposure to the extent of about half a stop (50%) will be corrected during development.

The increase of speed, in terms of Scheiner, resulting from the treatment is shown in the following example: a film of 32° Sch. and given pre-exposure treatment can be regarded as having an exposure speed of 35° Sch. If, after exposure, there will be time to give further treatment, the film may be regarded as having an exposure speed of about 36·5° Sch.

Roll-film Sizes

Description of film-size	Code Numbers	No. of exposures	Picture size (approximate)
			(in.)
35-mm. . .		50	1×1
			(24×24 mm.)
		36	$1 \times 1\frac{1}{2}$
			(24×36 mm.)
Bantam . .	88, 828	8	$1\frac{1}{8} \times 1\frac{5}{8}$
			(28×40 mm.)
Vest-Pocket .	27, 127, A8	8	$1\frac{5}{8} \times 2\frac{1}{2}$
		or	
		12	$1\frac{5}{8} \times 1\frac{5}{8}$
		or	
		16	$1\frac{5}{8} \times 1\frac{1}{8}$

Roll-film Sizes (*continued*)

Description of film-size	Code Numbers	No. of exposures	Picture size (approximate)
2¼–3¼	20, 120, B2 *or* 62, 620, Z20*	8 *or* 12 *or* 16	2¼ × 3¼ — 2¼ × 2¼ — 2¼ × 1⅝
2½–4¼	16, 116	8	2½ × 4¼
¼-plate	118, 130	6	3¼ × 4¼

The 62, 620, Z20 group is of the same size as the 20, 120, B2 group, but the spools are different; some cameras will take both types of spool, others will not.

Plate, Cut-film and Film-pack Sizes

Description of Plate size	Picture size (approx.)	Description of Plate size	Picture size (approx.)
	(in.)		(in.)
	1¾ × 2 5/16		20 × 30
Miniature Lantern	2 × 2		24 × 30
2¼–3¼	*†2¼ × 3¼		34 × 36
Standard Lantern	3¼ × 3¼		30 × 40
¼-plate	*†3¼ × 4¼		*Metric sizes*
Postcard	†3½ × 5½		(cm.)
	4 × 5		4·5 × 6
½-plate	†4¾ × 6½		6 × 9
Whole-plate	†6½ × 8½		9 × 12
	8 × 10		10 × 15
	10 × 12		13 × 18
	12 × 15		18 × 24
	16 × 18		24 × 30
	16 × 20		30 × 40
	20 × 24		40 × 50
			50 × 60

* Usual film-pack sizes.   † Usual cut-film sizes.

(*Note:* Sizes larger than whole-plate and 13 × 18 cm. are usually unobtainable except on special order.)

Colour Material: Generally as roll film in all sizes except 118, and as cut film in the following sizes: $2\frac{1}{2} \times 3\frac{1}{2}$ in.; $3\frac{1}{4} \times 3\frac{1}{4}$ in.; $3\frac{1}{4} \times 4\frac{1}{4}$ in.; 4×5 in.; $4\frac{3}{4} \times 6\frac{1}{2}$ in.; 9×12 cm.

Picture Dimensions: Conversion Tables

Inches	Centimetres*	Inches	Centimetres*
1	2·5	15	38·1
$1\frac{1}{8}$	2·8	$15\frac{3}{4}$	40·0
$1\frac{1}{2}$	3·8	16	40·6
$1\frac{5}{8}$	4·1	18	45·7
2	5·1	20	50·8
$2\frac{1}{4}$	5·7	24	61·0
$2\frac{1}{2}$	6·3	30	76·2
$2\frac{3}{4}$	7·0	36	91·4
3	7·6	40	101·6
$3\frac{1}{4}$	8·2		
$3\frac{1}{2}$	8·8	Centimetres	Inches†
$3\frac{3}{4}$	9·5		
4	10·2	2·4	1
$4\frac{1}{4}$	10·8	3·6	$1\frac{1}{2}$
$4\frac{1}{2}$	11·4	4·5	$1\frac{3}{4}$
$4\frac{3}{4}$	12·0	6	$2\frac{3}{8}$
5	12·7	9	$3\frac{1}{2}$
$5\frac{1}{8}$	13·0	10	4
$5\frac{1}{2}$	14·0	12	$4\frac{3}{4}$
6	15·2	13	$5\frac{1}{8}$
$6\frac{1}{2}$	16·5	15	$5\frac{7}{8}$
$7\frac{1}{8}$	18·0	18	$7\frac{1}{8}$
8	20·3	24	$9\frac{1}{2}$
$8\frac{1}{2}$	21·6	30	$11\frac{3}{4}$
$9\frac{1}{2}$	24·0	40	$15\frac{3}{4}$
10	25·4	50	$19\frac{5}{8}$
$11\frac{3}{4}$	30·0	60	$23\frac{5}{8}$
12	30·5		

* To nearest tenth.   † To nearest eighth.

SOURCES OF LIGHT

THE EFFECTIVE light for photographic purposes is that which, after passing through the camera lens and any filter, strikes the negative material. This light must, ideally, always be constant for the speed of negative material used.

Light outside the camera is very far from constant, however, and it is the purpose of the serious photographer who aims at correct exposure (and hence, consistent negatives) to modify the outside light as it passes through his shutter so that at the moment it reaches the negative material it is of correct value.

Broadly, outside light is divided into two groups: daylight and artificial light.

Daylight

Daylight is constantly varying in intensity, and its actinic value in terms of photography depends upon the following circumstances:

(i) *Latitude* (the light is brighter in the tropics than it is in, say, 50° N.—Britain, and Central Europe north of Italy and south of Scandinavia);

(ii) *Time of Year* (in Britain, light is brighter in June than it is in December);

(iii) *Time of Day* (light is brighter at midday than it is at 6 a.m. or 6 p.m.); and

(iv) *Sky Conditions* (light is brighter when the sky is clear than when it is clouded).

All of these variables are dealt with at once by exposure meters, for it is a characteristic of these meters to measure the light actually present at the moment of measurement.

The variables must be taken into account when using an exposure calculator or exposure tables, however; and to simplify the procedure the variables are grouped in the following way:

(i) Latitude. The calculator or tables are calibrated in advance by the designers for the latitude in which they are likely to be used.

(ii) Time of Year. The following three groups of months are considered to have light of equal values: May, June, July and August; September, October, March and April; November, December, January and February.

(iii) Time of day. The following groups of times are considered to have light of equal values: 10 a.m. to 3 p.m.; 8 a.m. to 10 a.m. and 3 p.m. to 6 p.m.; 7 a.m. to 8 a.m. and 6 p.m. to 7 p.m. (These times are Greenwich Mean Time; appropriate adjustments must be made for Summer Times.)

(iv) Sky Conditions. These are grouped as follows: Clear sun with white clouds; clear sun with blue sky; hazy sun (just strong enough to cast shadows); no sun (bright but sun obscured); dull (overcast).

It will be seen that this grouping will result in exposures which are not always theoretically correct, but such is the exposure-latitude of negative materials (especially roll films) that very acceptable results are obtained in practice.

Light Reflected from Subject

All calculations of the actinic value of light are based upon average subject, that is to say upon a subject which does not offer extremes of light and shade. But it has to be remembered that it is not the daylight itself which is photographed, but the light which is reflected into the camera lens (and so on to the negative material) by the subject itself.

Thus if the subject is a very light one (such as a white-washed cottage), it will reflect a great deal of the daylight measured according to the above rules; on the other hand, if the subject is dark (say a close up of a black dog) it will reflect comparatively little of that light.

There is a further consideration. The whole picture taken in by the camera lens may consist of reflected light which varies greatly in value according to whether individual components of the picture are light or dark; in this case the effective reflected light must be considered as coming from that part of the picture in which the photographer requires most detail.

Exposure meters solve the problem of subject very readily

for if the meter is held fairly close to that part of a subject in which most detail is required (say the shadow side of a face), it will at once indicate correct exposure for that part.

With calculators and tables some sort of estimation must be made, however, and to simplify the procedure a method of grouping is again resorted to. This grouping and its results upon exposure may be best demonstrated by the following list.

Variation of Exposure for Subject

Normal Subjects (no variation of exposure). Groups in open, buildings of average colour, landscapes with foliage, wide streets.

Light Subjects. Buildings of light colour, open landscapes, any scene with large light objects in the foreground ($\frac{1}{2}$ exposure required for normal subject). White buildings, very distant landscapes, beach scenes, snow scenes, any scene with large white objects in the foreground ($\frac{1}{4}$ exposure required for normal subject). Open sea and sky scenes, scenes from mountains or aeroplanes ($\frac{1}{8}$ exposure required for normal subject). Clouds ($\frac{1}{16}$ exposure required for normal subjects).

Dark Subjects. Buildings of dark colour, narrow streets, medium close-ups of people, any scene with fairly dark objects in foreground (twice exposure required for normal subjects). Head-and-shoulder portraits, close-ups of animals, scenes in moderate shade, any scene with very dark objects in foreground (4 times exposure required for normal subjects). Any scene in heavy shade (8 to 16 or more times exposure required for normal subjects).

All the above subjects are assumed to be in the open. If any of them are being photographed indoors, the following increases of exposure appropriate to the subject will be necessary:

Subjects close to window receiving direct light from sky: decorations light, as for moderate shade above; decorations dark, as for heavy shade above.

Subjects away from window: decorations light, about 16 times exposure appropriate to subject; decorations dark, 30 to 60 times exposure appropriate to subject. (*Note:* in any subject taken indoors away from a window, a useful rule-of-thumb method of determining exposure is to work out the exposure for subject for the open and multiply the result by 60; i.e. regard seconds as minutes.)

Lens Aperture

The lens aperture to be used for any particular picture is to a large extent at the choice of the photographer; but he is restricted in that choice by two considerations:

(i) If the light is poor and he must expose at a comparatively high shutter speed, he must use a large aperture;

(ii) If he requires considerable depth of focus (i.e. if he requires both foreground and background sharp) he must use a small aperture.

High shutter speeds are necessary when action pictures are being made and when the camera is being held in the hand at the time of exposure.

Large apertures are necessary when the foreground is required to be sharp and the background is required to be out of focus (this applies particularly to close-up portraits).

The selection of aperture and shutter speed in these special cases must always be a matter of compromise and must, in the last resort, depend upon the judgment of the photographer for best results. Where the light is very good, a wide choice is available; where the light is poor, the choice is considerably restricted.

For the values of apertures in terms of exposures, see page 20. For notes on shutter speeds, see page 33. For increase of exposure necessitated by the use of filters, see page 37.

An exposure table for daylight is given on the front endpaper of this book.

Artificial Light

The principal sources of artificial light for photography are as follow:

Tungsten Normal. This term covers all light emitted by half-watt lamps, whether of the household variety (up to about 150 watts) or of the floodlight variety (200 watts up to 1000 watts or more).

Tungsten Over-run. In this category the light is obtained from high-efficiency lamps of comparatively short life, who filaments are greatly overloaded by normal electricity supply sources. Examples of such lamps are: Photoflood I (275 watts over-run to give light equivalent to about 800 watts of tungsten normal, with life of about 2 hours); Photoflood II (500 watts over-run to give light equivalent to about 1500 watts of tungsten normal; life about 7 hours); and Photopearl (500 watts over-run to give about 800 watts of tungsten normal; life about 100 hours). The Photofloods are mainly useful in the home and in portrait studios where sessions are comparatively short; the Photopearl is better for commercial studios where the light is required for long periods.

Flashbulb. This source of light is the modern replacement of the old flash-powder (now practically obsolete). Flash-bulbs emit high-intensity light of very short duration (about $\frac{1}{25}$ to $\frac{1}{200}$ sec.), and are generally fired by battery, although some are made to fire from the mains. Because of their speed, flashbulbs are suitable for synchronisation with the camera shutter. Further notes on flash bulbs appear later.

Electronic Flashtube. This source is of somewhat higher brilliance and of much shorter duration (about $\frac{1}{5000}$ sec. for general photography) than the flashbulb. Specialised types are made with a flash-duration of one-millionth sec. The flashtube requires for its operation at least 2000 volts, which is supplied by means of a special power pack drawing energy from batteries, accumulators or (in the case of studio models) the mains. The battery and accumulator models are portable.

Tungsten Mains Supplies

It is important when using tungsten lamps of any kind to be assured that the mains supplying the current will not be overloaded. Current flowing in such mains is measured in amperes (*abb.* = amps.), and the following ratings are usual in domestic premises:

Wall-plugs for portable lights (standard lamps, etc.), 2 amps.
Points for permanent lights, irons, small vacuum cleaners, etc., 5 amps.
Power points for electric kettles, small heaters, etc., 10 amps.
Power points for large heaters, cookers, etc., 15 amps.
The wiring to the points mentioned above will stand some

overload, but the fuses in the fuse-box (if of correct value) will not. Since fuses are safety devices, no attempt should be made to put in any of higher value than the wiring is designed to carry.

To determine whether lamps used in photography are safe for the mains or not, a simple calculation is necessary. To find the amps. drawn from the mains by any lamp, divide its wattage by the volts of the supply. Thus if the supply is at 230 volts, a 100-watt lamp will draw 0·43 amps. approximately and four such lamps could safely be used on a 2-amp. circuit. At the same mains voltage, a Photoflood I (275 watts) would draw about 1·2 amps. and only one should be used on a 2-amp circuit, but four could be used on a 5-amp. circuit.

Flashbulb Data

The firing of single flashbulbs is usually effected by means of small batteries, two of which are connected in series to give 3 volts. The size of cell is the U2 (as used in the larger electric torches); more certainty of firing is obtained if the U2 Photoflash cells, specially developed for flashbulb work, are used.

A new development is the firing of flashbulbs by means of a $22\frac{1}{2}$-volt battery aided by a capacitor. This method is claimed to give more positive firing when using high-speed synchronisers.

Flashbulbs are available having a wide range of characteristics, the most important being that the bulb shall match the type of shutter and the timing of synchronisation of the shutter release. Focal-plane shutters, because of the comparatively long time taken for the slit to pass across the face of the negative material, require the use of bulbs which have a long peak flash. Further, most bulbs take about $\frac{1}{50}$ sec. after the current is applied to reach peak flash; hence the synchroniser should make contact slightly in advance of the shutter release. A few bulbs (called Speed Midgets—marked SM) fire almost at once, their total life from contact through flash to black being about $\frac{1}{200}$ sec., and in this case the shutter must open practically at the time of contact.

All flashbulbs may be used on the "open flash" system; that is, the shutter is opened, the bulb fired, and the shutter then closed.

Opposite is a table of flashbulb characteristics which will

assist in the selection of a suitable bulb for any particular set of circumstances.

Flashbulb Table

Bulb	Colour*	Flash	Firing	Total light	Best use
SM .	Clear	$\frac{1}{100}$	Immediate	Small	Open flash close-up
PF.14 . No. 5	Not Yellow	$\frac{1}{15}$	Delay	Small	Sync. close-up and general home use
PF.25 .	All	$\frac{1}{15}$	Delay	Medium	Press
PF.45 .	All	$\frac{1}{25}$	Delay	Medium	Focal plane
PF.60 . No. 22	All	$\frac{1}{15}$	Delay	Large	General studio
PF.100	All	$\frac{1}{15}$	Delay	Very large	Exteriors

* The colours are clear, blue, and yellow. Clear is used for general black-and-white photography; blue for daylight colour film; yellow for artificial light colour film. For those who do not wish to stock flashbulbs of different colours, there are stains made into which clear bulbs may be dipped for the colour required.

Notes:

1. Exposure data for the above flashbulbs are to be found in the section of Exposure. The bulb most generally suitable for amateur use is the PF.14 or No. 5; it is small, comparatively inexpensive, and reliable on all general synchronising systems.

2. As a general rule, if synchronisation is to be with fairly slow speeds (say $\frac{1}{25}$ sec.) on diaphragm shutters, short-peak bulbs ($\frac{1}{75}$ sec. or faster) should be used; if very high shutter speeds are necessary, press or focal-plane type bulbs should be used to allow for minor errors of synchronisation.

3. Any clear flashbulb may be specially lacquered for use with infra-red material, but since light-emission through the lacquer is low, the larger bulbs (PF.60 or No. 22) are best for this purpose.

4. Flashbulbs are expendable; a bulb cannot be used more than once.

5

Electronic Flashtube

This apparatus is suitable mainly for photographers who have to undertake a considerable amount of flash work. The matter is one of economy. An electronic flashtube will give some 10,000 flashes before requiring replacement, the cost of the tube being some £5; 10,000 flashbulbs of PF.14 type would cost £500, more than sufficient to cover the high capital cost of flashtube equipment.

The apparatus is further suitable for photographers whose work demands the freezing of fast action, the flash being of some $\frac{1}{5000}$ sec. average.

The strength of the flash, in terms of energy expended by the tube, is measured in joules, and the equipment for average use is 100 joules. Manufacturers of apparatus give fullest details concerning exposure, but in the absence of these the exposure may be reckoned as the same as for a PF.14 or No. 5 flashbulb working at a shutter speed of $\frac{1}{250}$ sec.

Batteries need replacement, and accumulators need re-charging at intervals. Batteries are relatively light but more expensive on replacement; they are generally used in 50-joule apparatus, giving about 100 flashes per replacement. Accumulators are used for higher-power apparatus (100 and 200 joules), giving about 200 flashes per charge. Apparatus above 200 joules is more conveniently powered from the mains.

General Notes on Equipment

The usual rule is to direct all sources of artificial light on to the subject by means of reflectors of polished metal, and most exposure data is based upon the assumption that this is done. Flashbulbs and flashtubes are nearly always used in reflectors, which generally form part of the apparatus designed to be mounted on the camera.

In the case of tungsten lamps of any type, polished metal reflectors are used on the basis of one per lamp, stands being obtainable which make possible the use of lamp-reflector units either singly or in banks for floodlight effects.

Where the bare lamp in a reflector is found to give too hard a light, resulting in harsh shadows, it may be softened by fixing to it (or placing between lamp and subject in some other way) a diffusing screen made of glass or thin fabric such as muslin or a linen handkerchief.

In place of polished metal reflectors, white card may be used, in which case it is usual to give double the exposure.

If the source of light is used in a living-room or studio whose walls and general furnishings are of light colour, it may be used without any reflector whatsoever, in which case the exposure is usually reckoned to be four times that necessary for a lamp in polished reflector.

The use of a diffusing screen calls for doubling the exposure.

These considerations are apart from the fact that the strength of any light falling upon a subject is in inverse proportion to the square of the distance from the source of that light. Thus if a source of light is 2 ft. from a subject and is given the arbitrary value of 1, the value will only be $\frac{1}{4}$ at 4 ft., only $\frac{1}{9}$ at 6 ft. and only $\frac{1}{16}$ at 8 ft.; conversely it would be 4 at 1 ft.

In the matter of over-run tungsten lamps, since their life is so short in many cases, and since they generate considerable heat while burning, they should be switched off between exposures. If it is necessary to keep them on during posing, either the longer life type should be used, or the lamps should be wired through a "series-parallel switch" so that, between exposures, only one-half the voltage is applied to the filaments. Series parallel switches are supplied by dealers, or may be made up by any electrician.

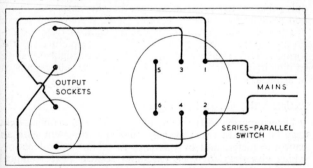

SERIES-PARALLEL SWITCH CONNECTIONS

A series-parallel switch, 2 plug sockets, a baseboard and wire are needed. When contact 3 is connected to 1, and 4 to 2, lamps are in parallel (full strength); when 3 is connected to 5 and 4 to 6, lamps are in series (half strength)

Using Artificial Light

The essential difference between artificial light and daylight is that, while daylight is continually varying, artificial light is constant and controllable. It must be kept in mind, however, that the light striking the surface of the negative material within the camera must still be constant and appropriate to the speed of the particular material used. Thus, while considerations related to the variation of light source by season, time of day, etc., may now be disregarded, the notes above on light reflected from subject, variations of exposure for subject, lens aperture and shutter speed still hold good.

When using artificial light, therefore, the following points must be taken into account when determining exposure:

(i) Sensitivity of negative material to artificial light;
(ii) The actinic value of the light;
(iii) The angle at which the light falls upon the subject; and
(iv) The amount of light reflected by the subject.

Sensitivity of Negative Material

Reference to the table on page 53 will show that the responses of negative material to daylight and artificial light are different. As a rough rule, orthochromatic materials have only $\frac{1}{4}$ the sensitivity to artificial light that they have to daylight, and panchromatic materials have $\frac{1}{2}$. If, therefore, a source of artificial light were as strong as daylight, increases of exposure would have to be made when taking pictures by the former. This is because negative materials are highly sensitive to blue light, which is plentiful in daylight but almost absent in artificial light.

Actinic Value of Artificial Light

Determination of the value of any source of artificial light may be made in two ways: by direct measurement with an exposure meter, and by reference to tables and calculators which give data for each particular source. The technical methods used to compile such tables or devise such calculators are not described here, but it should be noted that, in practice, the actinic value of light emitted by, say, a 100-watt tungsten lamp or a Photoflood I is practically constant. It tends to fall off a little as the lamp ages, but this consideration is not of great importance in black-and-white photography. For its effect in colour photography, see page 145.

The strength of light falling upon a subject is inversely proportional to the square of the distance of the subject from the source of the light, and an example of the effect of this law is given on page 67.

Where the source of artificial light is steady, as it is in the case of tungsten lighting, exposure details may readily be obtained from meters, calculators and tables, and the table to be found on the back endpaper of this book will serve as a reliable guide.

Where the source is of very brief duration, however, as it is in the case of flashbulbs and flashtubes, meters are of no help, and it is customary to obtain correct exposure by the use of what are referred to as flash-factors. A flash-factor is a figure which is a combination of aperture, distance and time; it takes into account (i) the strength of the flash from any particular make of bulb or rating of tube, (ii) the duration of that flash, (iii) the speed of the shutter (which may admit either the whole of the flash or only part of it), (iv) the distance from the source of the flash to the subject being photographed, (v) the aperture, and (vi) negative-material speed.

In use, the photographer selects a source of flash (a constant as to strength and duration of light), the negative material, a shutter-speed and the distance, leaving as his only variable the aperture or size of lens opening.

The following table, which includes data upon the flash-bulbs mentioned on page 65, and the notes accompanying it, will make the method of determining correct exposure for flashbulbs clear. (See overleaf for notes on the table.)

Flash-factors

Flashbulb	24° Sch.			27° Sch.			30° Sch.		
	OF	$\frac{1}{100}$	$\frac{1}{200}$	OF	$\frac{1}{100}$	$\frac{1}{200}$	OF	$\frac{1}{100}$	$\frac{1}{200}$
SM . .	55	55	40	70	70	55	95	95	75
PF.14 No. 5.	70	50	35	100	80	65	140	100	80
PF.25 .	90	65	45	160	110	80	230	160	110
PF.45 .	—	45	25	—	60	40	—	80	60
PF.60 No. 22	150	120	95	200	170	135	300	200	170
PF.100 .	200	—	—	270	—	—	380	—	—

Notes on Flash Factor Table:

Where no flash-factor is shown, bulbs are not recommended for use at the shutter-speeds indicated.

OF = Open Flash (i.e. open the shutter, fire the flash, close the shutter).

Fractions are shutter-speeds in seconds, the shutter to be so synchronised that it is fully open at peak-flash.

To find lens aperture to be used, enter table at bulb selected and note flash-factor under speed of negative material and shutter-speed. Then determine distance in feet between flash and subject, and divide it into flash-factor; the result will be the aperture to be used.

Example: Using a No. 5 bulb at Open Flash with Super XX (speed by artificial light 30° Sch.), the distance from flash to subject is found to be 9 ft. Since flash-factor is 140, aperture to be used is $140 \div 9 = f.$ 16 approx.

Flash factors for electronic flashtubes are supplied by the manufacturers.

Angle of Light

All exposures for sources of artificial light are based upon the assumption that the light is on the camera (i.e. dead in front of the subject) or at an angle of not more than 45° from that position. If the light is more than 45° and less than 70° off, double the exposure by making the shutter-speed slower or the lens aperture larger; if the light is between 70° and 90° off, quadruple the exposure.

Light Reflected by Subject

The exposures are further based upon the assumption that the subject is of medium colouring. If it is lighter or darker than medium, vary the exposure according to the details given on page 61.

Reflectors

The exposures are yet again based upon the assumption that the source of artificial light is used in a polished reflector. If it is used with white card, double the exposure; if it is used without any reflection whatsoever, quadruple the exposure.

LIGHTING FOR PORTRAITURE

It is assumed in diagrams 1 to 4 below that Photofloods in reflectors are used. Diagram 5 shows lighting for more versatile equipment.

Heights and distances-away of lamps are matters for adjustment when the sitter, S, is in position. The main light, ML, should as a general rule be 12 to 18 in. higher than the sitter's head; back lights, BL, can be up to 4 ft. higher, and may be diffused if too strong.

Other abbreviations are: BG, background; BGL, background light; FL, 500 to 1000 watt floodlight; R, white reflector; SL, secondary (fill in) light

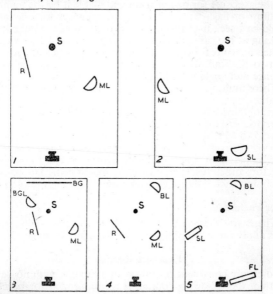

1. Simple arrangement with 1 lamp and white reflector for filling in.

2. Using 2 lamps, shadows cast by ML being lighted by SL.

3. The second lamp, BGL, used to give a light background.

4. The second lamp, BL, set high, used to light the hair.

5. A common studio arrangement, the main light being a powerful flood, the secondary light being a diffused spot.

Diffusers

If a diffuser is placed between the source of artificial light and the subject, double the exposure. Note that if a linen handkerchief is used as a diffuser, it might be necessary to increase exposure by ×3 or ×4.

Multiple Sources

Where more than one source of artificial light is used (i.e. two or more lamps or flashes in combination), and they are all of the same type and at the same distance and angle, work out the exposure for one of them and divide it by the number of lamps or flashes used. Thus if the exposure for one lamp would be $\frac{1}{5}$ sec., the exposure for two lamps of the same kind working at the same distance and angle would be $\frac{1}{10}$ sec.; if the lens aperture for one flashbulb were $f.$ 16, the lens aperture for two flashbulbs of the same kind working at the same distance and angle would be $f.$ 22.

Where multiple sources of artificial light are used and they are at different distances or of different types, correct exposure is best obtained by meter. A rough rule is to find the exposure appropriate to the principal light working alone and to shorten it by 25 to 50% for each additional lamp used.

In working out exposure for multiple sources, account must also be taken of angle of light, light reflected by subject, reflectors and diffusers, as previously mentioned. Lamps used purely for back-lighting or background lighting are ignored.

Filter Factors

Where any filter is used over the camera lens, the same rules apply for artificial light as for daylight (see page 37).

Exposure Routine

To ensure consistent operation of a camera, with no detail omitted, the following routine is recommended for practice with an empty camera until it becomes automatic.

* Note that steps 2, 3, 4, 5 and 6 may not be necessary or possible with cheaper cameras.

1. Sight and compose subject in viewfinder.
*2. Set focus.
*3. Set stop for depth of focus required.

*4. Set shutter-speed appropriate to light and stop.

*5. Cock shutter.

*6. Re-sight subject in viewfinder.

7. Release shutter.

8. Wind on film or change plateholder in readiness for next exposure.

Where it is intended to take general "candid" or newsy pictures (in which speed of operation of the camera is essential) the camera may be preset as follows: focus at 18 ft.; stop at f.11; shutter-speed at $\frac{1}{25}$ sec.; shutter cocked. This presetting (which is similar to the permanent settings of many box cameras) will bring everything into focus from about 10 ft. to infinity, and is suitable for average bright daylight (winter months excepted) with negative material of 28° Sch. and faster.

If close-ups under similar conditions are intended, the focus preset can be at 10 ft., when (the other presets being the same as given above) focus will be from about 7 ft. to about 17 ft. If distances nearer than about 7 ft. are contemplated, the depth of field tables (pages 25 to 29) should be consulted.

Note re Reflex Cameras: Steps 1, 2 and 6 will be a composite operation while looking at the subject in the viewfinder.

Before any camera with a cocking shutter is put away after resetting, the shutter should be released, either in total darkness or when the camera is empty.

SPECIAL EXPOSURE PROBLEMS

Action Pictures

THE shutter speed necessary to arrest the movement of a moving object so that it will not appear blurred on prints depends upon the following considerations:

(i) The speed of the object;

(ii) The distance of the object from the lens;

(iii) The direction of movement of the object in relation to the lens;

(iv) The focal length of the lens; and

(v) The degree of enlargement of the final print.

Since all these considerations cannot conveniently be incorporated in one table, the first three are included in the table immediately following, while factors which will allow for (iv) and (v) are shown separately.   Shutter speeds are in seconds.

Speed (m.p.h.)	Examples	Distance (ft.)	Shutter speeds		
			1	2	3
2	Street scenes, landscapes, general outdoor shots with no rapid motion	25	$\frac{1}{5}$	$\frac{1}{10}$	$\frac{1}{25}$
3	Pedestrians, cattle	25	$\frac{1}{25}$	$\frac{1}{50}$	$\frac{1}{100}$
10	Cyclists in streets, yachts, children at play, swimmers, rowing boats, foliage in light breeze	25	$\frac{1}{100}$	$\frac{1}{200}$	$\frac{1}{300}$
20	Motor vehicles in streets, track events, steamers, boxing, skating	25	$\frac{1}{150}$	$\frac{1}{300}$	$\frac{1}{500}$
30	Horse and cycle racing, speed boats, trains, diving, ball games, flying birds	25	$\frac{1}{250}$	$\frac{1}{500}$	$\frac{1}{1000}$

Shutter speeds: Column 1 refers to objects moving directly towards or away from the camera; column 2 to objects moving obliquely towards or away from the camera; and column 3 to objects moving across the camera right-to-left or left-to-right.

Notes: As a general rule, movement is not arrested well at distances less than 25 ft., although slow-moving objects (2-m.p.h.) can be attempted at 15 ft., when half the exposure stated above can be given.   For longer distances than 25 ft. the rule is: double the distance, double the exposure.

In certain cases an effect of speed can be given by swinging the camera at the time of exposure, the rate of swing being such that the image of the principal subject to be photographed is held in the middle of the viewfinder. The result of such swing is to arrest the movement of the subject while blurring the background.

Corrections for Focal Length

Find the focal length of the lens used, and multiply the exposures given opposite by the appropriate factor.

Focal length (cm.) .	3·5	5	7·5	10	12·5	15
Factor . . .	2	1½	1	¾	⅗	½

Corrections for Enlargement

Multiply the exposures given opposite by the factor appropriate to the degree of enlargement required.

Degree of enlargement .	Contact	×5	×10	×15
Factor	1	½	⅓	⅕

Difficult Lighting Conditions

Some workers recommend the following variations in normal technique where prevailing light may be unsuitable for good results ordinarily.

Where lighting is so harsh that highlights will appear "burnt out" and shadows will show no detail: double exposure time and halve development time.

Where lighting is very flat (as on dull days): halve exposure time, and increase time of development by 25 to 50 per cent.

In figure photography by artificial light: halve exposure time and give very full development.

Interiors by Daylight

In the absence of an exposure meter which will read down far enough for very weak light, the correct exposure for interiors must of necessity be approximate. It is generally the case that normal negatives are the exception, but that if negative stock with wide latitude is chosen, excellent results can be achieved by normal development and by selecting a suitable grade of paper when printing.

The following table will give a reasonable indication of exposure for daylight provided that the window is of moderate size and is not overshadowed by trees, buildings or other obstructions to light.

The figures are based upon the following factors: speed of negative material, about 29° Sch.; stop f. 11; time, 3 hours each side of noon; only one window. Times given are in seconds.

Decoration of walls: colour of hangings	Clear sky	Hazy sky	Cloudy	Dull
White, broken white, cream; blues and yellows	3	8	15	30
Buff, light green, light grey, and other medium colours; hangings similar .	6	15	30	60
Panelling, reds, and other heavy colours; dark	18	45	90	180

(*Note:* For 2 windows, multiply by the factor $\frac{2}{3}$; for windows, multiply by the factor $\frac{1}{2}$.)

Negative Groups (Development)

(*See formulae for ID-2 and D-76 on pages 84–5. and negative materials list pages 53–4*).

Agfa: Isochrom F (IV); Isopan F (IV); Isopan FF (I); Isopan ISS (VI).

Barnet: FG Pan (II); Presstopan (III); Sensichrome (V); SS Ortho (V); Super Press (IV); Ultrapan (IV).

Dufay: Ortho (V); Pan (IV).

Ferrania: P3 (IV); S2 (IV); Super Panchro (VI); Ultrachromatica (V).

Gevaert: Microgran (III — plates IV); Panchromosa (V); Superchrom (V).

Ilford: Commercial Ortho (IV); FP3 (VI); FP Special (V); HP3 (V); Iso Zen (VI); Press Ortho (IV); Selochrome (V); SG Pan (VI); SR Pan (II).

Kodak: Commercial Ortho (IV); O.250 (I); O.800 (III); Ortho X (V); P.300 (II); P.1200 (V); P.1500 (II); Panatomic X (IV); Plus X (V); Super XX (V); Verichrome (IV).

Part Three

THE DARKROOM

DARKROOM EQUIPMENT

These items are indispensable

Development of Negative Material

*Developing Tank	For either roll film or plates and cut film; may be adjustable for size within limits; for roll film may have a "self-loading" device. Models are available which may be loaded entirely in daylight.
Developing Dishes (3)	If development is to be by dish instead of tank. Dishes should be fairly deep, and of about twice the size of the material usually handled.
Thermometer	To read from about 40° to 90°F.
Graduated Measure	Glass; capacity 20 fluid ounces.
Stirring Rod	Glass, with "crusher" end.
Funnel	Glass, to fit filling aperture of tank.
Filter Paper, or Cotton Wool	For use with funnel to filter processing solutions.
Timing Device	Clock or watch with seconds-hand, or special photographic timer.
Film Clips, or Drying Rack	Clips for roll or cut film (2 per roll; 1 per piece); rack for plates.
Rubber Gloves	Only essential for operators susceptible to developer poisoning.
Developer	To choice; ready-compounded, of size to suit quantity of work to be done.
Acid Fix	Ready-compounded, powder or liquid.

Hardener	Essential when drying is to be by heat; acid fix with hardener (ready-compounded) is recommended.
Stop Bath	Ready-compounded or as loose chemical, for use when development times are very short.
Storage Bottles (2)	Brown, ground-glass stoppers, of size to suit work being done.
Chemical Balance Weights Loose Chemicals	Balance about 8 oz. or 250 grammes capacity. (These items are required only if the operator prefers to compound his own developers, etc.)
Safelight	Lamp with safelight screens to suit negative material being handled (required where tank cannot be loaded in daylight).

Printing by Contact

*Printing Frame, or Printing Box	Of size to suit the largest print to be made; either item preferably with adjustable masks.
Printing Masks	Of various standard sizes if adjustable masks are not already on frame or box.
*Developing Dishes	If not already available for negatives.
*Safelight Screen	For contact papers; to fit lamp used for negatives.
*Printing Light	A 25- or 40-watt lamp, pearl or opal, in any convenient holder, with switch.
*Printing Paper	Surface and finish to taste; grade to suit negatives being printed.
*Developer	To suit contact papers, if negative developer is not of "universal" type.
*Print Clips	For hanging prints to dry; sufficient for number of prints likely to be handled in one session.
Ferrotype Plate Blotting Paper Squeegee	These items are necessary if prints are to be finished with a high-glazed surface.

Print Dryer   To suit electric mains, where prints are to be dried quickly by heat.

(*Note:* In addition, *Thermometer, *Graduated Measure, *Stirring Rod, *Timing Device, Rubber Gloves, *Acid Fix, Hardener, Stop Bath, Storage Bottles and Chemical Balance, etc. already mentioned in previous list.)

Printing by Projection

*Enlarger   Lighting system to choice of operator; lens and condenser for largest negative to be handled; baseboard for largest print normally made.

Developing Dishes (3)   Medium depth; comfortably larger than the largest print normally made.

Safelight Screens (2)   For bromide and chlorobromide papers; to fit lamp used for negatives or contact papers.

Printing Paper   Surface and finish to taste; grade to suit negatives being printed; sizes according to sizes of prints usually required.

Developer   To suit enlarging papers, if negative developer is not of "universal" type.

Dodging Devices   For "holding back" parts of the projected image during printing.

Foot Switch   Where switch fitted to enlarger is not considered convenient in operation.

Paper Trimmer   For prints of non-standard sizes, or for trimming out to improve composition.

Paper Holder   To take largest print normally made, with adjustable masking (if enlarger baseboard is not already fitted with paper holder).

(*Note:* In addition, *Print Clips, Ferrotype Plate, Blotting Paper, Squeegee, Print Dryer, *Thermometer, *Graduated Measure, *Stirring Rod, *Timing Device, Rubber Gloves, Acid Fix, Hardener, Stop Bath, Storage Bottles and Chemical Balance, etc.—included in previous lists.)

Notes on Darkroom Equipment

The above lists are based upon normal conditions; if negatives or prints need after-treatment of a chemical nature reference should be made to the sections on Negative Development and Printing later in this book for additional materials required.

In addition to the equipment mentioned in the lists above all processing calls for adequate washing arrangements, preferably with running water, such as a deep, clean sink or hand-basin.

Concerning timing devices for projection printing, an electronic timer can be obtained which, when set for the time of exposure, will automatically switch the enlarger on and off.

Enlargers are of two principal types: hand focusing and automatic focusing. The hand-focusing type requires focusing as a separate operation after the picture-size has been determined; the automatic focusing type maintains focus at all positions of the enlarger head without separate adjustment.

Where a hand-focusing enlarger is used, some sort of magnifier (a simple magnifying lens such as a reading glass, or a special enlarger-focuser) is of considerable help in getting sharp focus.

For the retouching of negatives, a set of retouching knives and leads or brushes and colour, together with some sort of retouching frame or desk for holding negatives, are essential.

NEGATIVE DEVELOPMENT

Principles of Development

A LATENT (invisible) image is formed on the negative emulsion in the course of exposure, the emulsion being affected by the light falling upon it in proportion to the strength of that light. Development is the process of making the image visible; fixation is the process of making the coloration of the image permanent.

Negative development in its broadest sense should be looked upon as a number of immediately successive processes as follows:

(i) Development to make the image visible to the desired degree of coloration (coloration in this sense meaning varying depths of black and grey on a clear background);

(ii) Stopping of development practically instantaneously by means of a stop bath in cases of short development times and processing at high temperatures;

(iii) Fixing the image so that unwanted parts of the emulsion are dissolved away and the remaining (developed) emulsion will no longer be affected by light; and finally

(iv) Washing from the emulsion all the chemicals remaining in it as a result of the above processes.

Developer Constituents

In practically all negative developers used in stage (i) there are five principal constituents:

The Reducing Agent, the function of which is to split up the silver halides, which form the sensitive part of the emulsion, so that metallic silver of various degrees of blackness is left in the emulsion. Examples of reducing agents are: metol, hydroquinone, pyro, amidol, paraphenylene-diamine, glycin, pyrocatechin and Meritol (the last a proprietary Johnson product).

The Accelerator, an alkali whose purpose is to accelerate the working of the reducing agent. Examples of accelerators are: sodium carbonate (in anhydrous and crystalline forms) and borax.

The Preservative, whose purpose is to preserve the reducing agent, which would otherwise oxidise while being worked in contact with the air. Examples of preservatives are: sodium sulphite (anhydrous or crystalline) and potassium meta-bisulphate.

The Restrainer, which holds back the activity of the reducing agent sufficiently so that it will reduce only that part of the silver halide in the emulsion which has been acted upon by light. Absence of restrainer from a development solution generally results in fog all over a negative. The most generally used restrainer is potassium bromide.

The Solvent, which is generally tap water containing a

6

number of substances of no importance to the process, except
that a large content of lime may leave a thin deposit on the
negative. This deposit may be dispersed after washing by
running the negative through a very weak solution (1%) of
citric or hydrochloric acid and rinsing off.

Development Method

The process of negative development is to some extent
variable, and contrast or softness can be controlled by the
selection of a suitable developer formula.

This apart, most modern workers aim at a standard normal
negative produced in a developer acting at a fixed temperature
for a fixed time; except for experimental purposes, the method
of development by inspection is practically obsolete.

Negative developers generally work best at 65°F., but where
for various reasons this exact temperature is not practicable
they may be used at temperatures between 55°F. and 75°F.
Some developers which do not contain hydroquinone may be
used a little below 55°F.; others, compounded for processing
under tropical conditions, may (sometimes must) be used at
temperatures above 75°F.

Standard times for developers are based upon about 65°F.
If the temperature is lower, the time must be increased; if the
temperature is higher, it must be decreased (see page 89).

The standard time of any developer depends principally
upon (i) the type of negative emulsion to be developed; and
(ii) the constituents and composition of the developer. A
further factor which will have a bearing upon the standard
time is the personal preference of the photographer in the
matters of contrast and printing density.

Desensitising

When, for experimental reasons, a negative or negatives
are to be developed by inspection, a desensitiser may be used
before or concurrently with development.

The two desensitisers most generally in use are pinacrypto
green and safranine, dyes which greatly reduce the sensitivity
of negative materials to light. They are not recommended
for use in the case of ultra-fine-grain development owing to
their great restraining influence on the reducing agent.

To use, the negative is bathed in a weak solution of the desensitiser in total darkness for 2 min. before being placed in the developer, or the desensitiser is added to the developer and the first 2 min. of development is carried out in total darkness. After this time, development may be by bright-orange light for non-panchromatic materials or by weak bright-green light for panchromatic materials.

Negative Developers

Before any development of negatives is undertaken, consideration should be given to the methods which are to be used in making the final prints. For example, if the prints are to be made by contact only (i.e. there is to be no enlargement), then grain is not of any particular importance and vigorous development can be used. Where enlargements are to be made, however, a gentler developer—one which will keep the grain in the negative fairly fine—must be employed.

To summarise these points, the following table gives recommendations of suitable developer types:

Degree of enlargement	Approx. limits of enlargement	Type of developer recommended
None or very slight . .	Same size to ×2	Normal
Slight . . .	×2 to ×5	Semi-fine grain
Moderate . . .	×5 to ×10	Fine grain
Considerable* . .	Above ×10	Ultra-fine grain

With considerable degrees of enlargement, it is further recommended that fine-grain negative stock also be used (see pages 36 and 53).

When using normal developers, some variation may be made to suit the subject. For example, a portrait taken by artificial light which is thought to have been a little hard could be developed in a soft-working normal developer; a picture which is thought to be somewhat under-exposed may be developed in a developer which will produce enhanced contrast.

Selection of a suitable developer can be made from the following pages.

List of Developers

(Note that most of the developers listed below can be pur-chased ready-compounded in either powder or liquid form. Inquiries should be made of suppliers.)

Normal Developer—General Use

Metol-Hydroquinone (ID-2)

Metol . . .	20 grains	1 gramme
Sodium sulphite (cryst.) .	3 oz.	75 grammes
Hydroquinone . . .	80 grains	4 grammes
Sodium carbonate (cryst.) .	2 oz.	50 grammes
Potassium bromide . .	20 grains	1 gramme
Water to make . . .	20 oz.	500 c.c.

Dissolve the chemicals in the order given. For dish development, dilute 1 part of the above with 2 parts of water for tank development dilute with 5 parts of water.

Times of development in min. at 65°F. are:

Strength	Negative group (see page 76)							
	I	II	III	IV	V	VI	VII	VIII
Dish .	$3\frac{1}{2}$	4	$4\frac{1}{2}$	5	6	$7\frac{1}{2}$	$8\frac{1}{2}$	10
Tank .	7	8	9	10	12	15	17	20

Normal Developer—Soft-working

Metol (ID-3)

Metol . . .	50 grains	2·5 grammes
Sodium sulphite (cryst.) .	1 oz.	25 grammes
Sodium carbonate (cryst.) .	2 oz.	50 grammes
Potassium bromide . .	10 grains	0·5 grammes
Water to make . . .	20 oz.	500 c.c.

Dissolve the chemicals in the order given. Dilute the above with 3 parts of water for both dish and tank use.

Time of development at 65°F., as for ID-2 tank strength or according to requirements.

Normal Developer—Vigorous

Pyro-Metol (ID–4)

Solution A

Metol . . .	35 grains	2 grammes
Potassium metabisulphite .	100 grains	6 grammes
Pyrogallic acid . .	100 grains	6 grammes
Water to make . . .	20 oz.	500 c.c.

Solution B

Sodium carbonate (cryst.) .	4 oz.	100 grammes
Water to make . . .	20 oz.	500 c.c.

Dissolve the chemicals in the order given, and keep the solutions separate until just before use. For use, mix equal parts of A and B.

Times of development at 65°F. are about half those shown for ID–2 dish strength.

Other normal developers recommended are: Ilford Certinal; Ilford ID–43 (high-speed developer for Press work); Johnson's Azol; Johnson's Universal; Kodak D–72; Tabloid Rytol.

Semi-fine-grain Developer—General Use

Elon-Hydroquinone-Borax (D–76)

Elon (Metol) . . .	17·5 grains	1 gramme
Sodium sulphite (cryst.) .	4 oz.	100 grammes
Hydroquinone . .	43·75 grains	2·5 grammes
Borax . . .	17·5 grains	1 gramme
Water to make . . .	20 oz.	500 c.c.

Dissolve the chemicals in the order given. Use without dilution.

Times of development in min. at 65°F. are:

Strength	Negative group (See page 76)							
	I	II	III	IV	V	VI	VII	VIII
Full .	9	10	11	14	17	19	22	25

Semi-fine-grain Developer—Tropical Use

Metol (*D–23*)

Elon (Metol)	.	115 grains	3·75 grammes
Sodium sulphite (cryst.)	.	7 oz.	100 grammes
Water to make	.	35 oz.	500 c.c.

Dissolve the chemicals in the order given, and use without dilution.

Development times at 65°F. as for D–76, or for about $3\frac{1}{2}$ to $7\frac{1}{2}$ min. up to 85°F. (maximum). When processing at high temperatures, a stop bath should be used between development and fixation.

Other semi-fine-grain developers recommended are: Edwal 10; Ilford MQ-Borax (ID–11); Johnson's Fine Grain; M. & B. Promicrol; Tabloid Fine Grain.

Fine-grain Developer—General Use

Metol-Kodalk (*DK–20*)

Elon (metol)	.	44 grains	2·5 grammes
Sodium sulphite (cryst.)	.	4 oz.	100 grammes
Kodalk	.	17·5 grains	1 gramme
Potassium thiocyanate	.	9 grains	0·5 gramme
Potassium bromide	.	4·5 grains	0·25 gramme
Water to make	.	20 oz.	500 c.c.

Dissolve the chemicals in the order given, and use without dilution.

Times of development at 65°F., as for D–76.

Fine-grain Developer—Tropical Use

Metol (*D–25*)

Elon (metol)	.	110 grains	3·75 grammes
Sodium sulphite (cryst.)	.	6 oz. 290 gr.	100 grammes
Sodium bisulphite	.	$\frac{1}{2}$ oz.	7·5 grammes
Water to make	.	35 oz.	500 c.c.

Dissolve the chemicals in the order given, and use without dilution.

Times of development at 65°F., about one-third longer than for D–76; or at about D–76 times for 80°F. (maximum).

When processing at high temperatures, a stop bath should be used between development and fixation.

Other fine-grain developers recommended are: Edwal 20; Ilford ID–48; Johnson's Meritol-Metol; Sease PDMG; Tabloid Fine Grain with Sulphite.

Ultra-fine-grain Developer

Sease III

Sodium sulphite (cryst.)	.	3¾ oz.	90 grammes
Paraphenylene diamine	.	91 grains	5 grammes
Glycin	. .	55 grains	3 grammes
Water to make	. .	20 oz.	500 c.c.

Dissolve the chemicals in hot water (about 120°F.) in the order given, and use without dilution.

Times of development in minutes at 65°F. are: for very slow films of very fine grain, 8; slow films of fine grain, 10; medium-speed films, 15; fast films, 25.

Other ultra-fine-grain developers recommended are: Johnson's Meritol Super Fine Grain; PAC Super Degrainol; Sease I; Sease ND3.

Bulk Tank Developers

The developers used for bulk development of negative materials are usually of the vigorous type, producing somewhat contrasty negatives which will result in "bright" prints. They are used with replenishers, for addition when the original solution begins to lose bulk.

A typical bulk tank developer with its replenisher is—

Pyro-MQ (ID–6)

Metol	. . .	1 oz.	25 grammes
Sodium sulphite (cryst.)	.	1¾ lb.	700 grammes
Sodium bisulphite	.	1 lb.	400 grammes
Hydroquinone	. .	5½ oz.	135 grammes
Pyrogallic acid	. .	1 oz.	25 grammes
Sodium carbonate (cryst.)	.	5 lb.	2 kilogram
Potassium bromide	.	50 grains	2 grammes
Water to make	. .	10 gal.	40 litres

Dissolve the chemicals in the order given in about 7 gal. warm water, and make up to 10 gal. with cold.

Pyro-MQ Replenisher (ID–6R)

Metol . . .	$\frac{1}{2}$ oz.	12·5 grammes
Sodium sulphite (cryst.) .	$\frac{1}{2}$ lb.	200 grammes
Sodium bisulphite .	$\frac{1}{4}$ lb.	100 grammes
Hydroquinone . . .	$1\frac{1}{2}$ oz.	37·5 grammes
Sodium carbonate (cryst.) .	$1\frac{1}{2}$ lb.	600 grammes
Water to make . .	1 gal.	4 litres

Dissolve the chemicals in the order given. Before adding to developer, dilute with an equal quantity of water.

Time of development for roll films averages about 10 min. at 65°F.; the time is varied according to condition of developer and type of film.

The above developer and replenisher is supplied by Ilford ready-compounded and packed to make 10 gal. or 12 gal. of the developer at working strength.

Two-bath Developers

In cases where fine grain is required but where exposure has been somewhat inadequate, or where some reduction of contrast is required, two-bath development (also referred to as "compensating development") is now popular.

The principle of this method is that the negative material is first immersed in a solution of reducing agent and preservative for a certain time—long enough for the emulsion to absorb sufficient of these chemicals. The material is then placed in a bath of accelerator, when development takes place; but since the reducing agent held in the emulsion becomes quickly exhausted in those parts which are fully exposed, and less rapidly exhausted in those parts which are less exposed, contrast is automatically reduced and full development does not give increase of grain.

A typical two-bath developer is that devised by Johnson and Sons. The formulæ are:

Johnson's Meritol-Caustic

First Bath

Meritol . . .	140 grains	8 grammes
Sodium sulphite (cryst.) .	3 oz. 260 gr.	90 grammes
Water to make . .	20 oz.	500 c.c.

Dissolve the chemicals in the order given; for use dilute with 4 parts of water.

Second Bath

Caustic Soda (10% sol.)	.	1 oz.	25 c.c.
Water to make .	. .	20 oz.	500 c.c.

On average, the film or plate is immersed in the first bath at 65°F. for 3 min.; then, without rinsing, plunged into the second bath at 65°F. for 3 min. Finally, without rinsing, it is placed in an acid fix for 5–10 min. and washed in the usual way. Fuller directions may be obtained from the manufacturers.

Other two-bath developers recommended are: Symon Two Bath (a variant of DK–20—see page 86); Stoeckler High Speed (for Press use, the total development time being about 2 min.).

Development Times at various Temperatures

Time given for 65°F.	*Development time for*						
	55°	60°	62·5°	68°	70°	72·5°	75°
1½	3	2¼	2		1¼		1
2	3½	2¾	2½	1¾	1½		1¼
3	5	4	3½	2¾	2½		1¾
4	6	5	4½	3½	3¼	3	2½
5	7¼	6¼	5½	4½	4¼	4	3¼
6	8½	7¾	6¾	5½	5¼	4¾	4
7	9¾	8½	7¾	6¼	5¾	5½	5
8	11	9½	8	7¼	6¾	6¼	5¾
9	13	11	9¾	8¼	7¾	7	6¼
10	15	12	11	9¼	8½	7¾	7¼
12	18	15	13½	11	10	9¼	8½
14	21	18	15¾	12½	11½	10½	9½
16	23	19½	17½	14½	13½	12¼	11
18	25½	22	20	16½	15½	13½	12¾
20	28	24	22	18½	17	15½	14
25	36	30	27	23	21	19½	18
30	45	36	33	27	25	23	21
35	50	43	38	32	29	26	24
40	57	48	44	37	34	31	28

All times given in table above are in min.

Notes on Development Times

Times of development vary according to the temperature at which any developer is used, the normal temperature being regarded as 65°F. Except in the case of developers specially compounded for tropical use, all developers work at their best between about 60° and 70°F., and in general developers should not be used cooler than 55°F. or warmer than 75°F.

Given the time of development at 65°F., recommended times for development at other temperatures will be found in the table on page 89.

Stop Bath

Where in cases of short development times, it is considered necessary to use an acid bath in place of a plain rinse in order to stop development immediately, the following formula is recommended:

Potassium metabisulphite .	$\frac{1}{2}$ oz.	12$\frac{1}{2}$ grammes
Water	20 oz.	500 c.c.

In the case of small negatives, or where processing is being carried on at temperatures above 70°F., a hardener may be added to the above bath ($\frac{1}{2}$ oz. chrome alum.).

Fixing Baths

The basis of all fixing baths for negative material is a 25% solution of hypo (sodium thiosulphate) and an acid fix is recommended. Where negatives are small, or where processing temperatures are above 70°F., an acid fix with hardener is recommended.

Acid Fix

Hypo	5 oz.	125 grammes
Potassium metabisulphite .	$\frac{1}{2}$ oz.	12$\frac{1}{2}$ grammes
Water	20 oz.	500 c.c.

Acid Fix with Hardener

Hypo	5 oz.	125 grammes
Potassium metabisulphite .	$\frac{1}{2}$ oz.	12$\frac{1}{2}$ grammes
Chrome alum . . .	$\frac{1}{2}$ oz.	12$\frac{1}{2}$ grammes
Water	20 oz.	500 c.c.

When compounding either of the above baths, dissolve the chemicals in the order given, each to be completely dissolved before the next is added.

Correction Formulæ

Chromium Intensifier

For cases of under-exposure and/or under-development. The process may be repeated if necessary.

First the soaked negative is bleached in

| Potassium bichromate. | . | 87·5 grains | 4·5 grammes |
| Water | . . . | 20 oz. | 500 c.c. |

to which is added immediately before use

| Hydrochloric acid (conc.) | . | 54·75 minims | 3·2 grammes |

The negative is bleached until there is no black visible, then washed in running water until all yellow has been cleared, leaving the emulsion a buff colour. The negative is now developed fully in a normal developer in full daylight or strong artificial light, washed for 30 min. (no fixing is necessary) and —if the degree of intensification is satisfactory—dried in the usual way.

(*Notes:* Fine-grain developers should *not* be used after a chromium bleach. If it is desired to reduce contrast during the intensification, some black may be left visible by stopping the bleaching process before full time, then washing and developing as stated above.)

Uranium Intensifier

A one-operation intensifier for cases of under-exposure; it produces quick results of limited permanence. Make two solutions:

Solution A

| Uranium nitrate. | . | . | 1 oz. | 25 grammes |
| Water to make . | . | . | 10 oz. | 250 c.c. |

Solution B

| Potassium ferricyanide | . | 1 oz. | 25 grammes |
| Water to make . | . | . | 10 oz. | 250 c.c. |

For use, mix 1 part of A, 1 part of B, 1 part of acetic acid (glacial), and 6 parts of water. The working solution does not keep once mixed.

Immerse the negative in the working solution and keep it there until the required degree of intensification is reached. The image becomes brown in colour.

Wash in a number of changes of *still* water until all yellow stain has gone.

If intensification has gone too far it may be removed by immersing the negative in a 5% solution of sodium carbonate and washing thoroughly. The intensification process may then be repeated to the required degree.

Farmer's Reducer

For cases of over-exposure with or without over-development, and to clear fog.

First make two separate solutions:

| (i) Hypo | . | . | . | . | 1 oz. |
| Water | . | . | . | . | 10 oz. |

| (ii) Potassium ferricyanide | . | 1 oz. |
| Water | . | . | . | . | 10 oz. |

When the negative to be treated is well soaked, mix 2 oz of solution (i) with $\frac{1}{4}$ oz. of solution (ii), immerse the negative in the mixture at once, keep it moving gently, watch it closely until the desired degree of reduction has been almost achieved then transfer it quickly to running water and wash for 15 min.

(*Notes:* The hypo solution must *not* be an acid fix. Local reduction of a negative can be achieved by dipping a piece of cotton wool into the mixed solutions, squeezing it out until it is just moist, and then dabbing with it the parts of the negative to be treated; reduction can be stopped for inspection by holding the negative under running water, and the dabbing can be repeated as desired. *The mixed solution is not effective after about 10 min.*)

Ammonium Persulphate Reducer

For cases of over-development of normal exposures, resulting in dense, contrasty negatives.

Ammonium persulphate	.	140 grains	7·5 grammes
Water to make	.	.	10 oz.	250 c.c.
Sulphuric acid (conc.).	.	5 minims	0·25 c.c.

Dissolve the chemicals in the order given, and use at once. Immerse the well-soaked negative in the solution and keep it moving until the required degree of reduction is reached. Then place the negative for 10 min. in a 5% solution of sodium sulphite; finally wash for 15 min.

Faults in Negatives

Fault	Cause	Remedy
Parts unsharp .	Faulty focus, or exposure too slow to stop action	None
All unsharp. .	Faulty focus, or camera shake	None
Two pictures superimposed	Two exposures on one frame	None
No detail in shadows	Insufficient exposure	Generally none
Some detail in shadows; negative thin	Insufficient exposure, or under-development or both	Use chromium intensifier
Detail good; negative thin	Under-development	Use chromium intensifier
Some detail in shadows; negative contrasty	Under-exposure and over-development	Reduce in ammonium persulphate, wash, and use chromium insifier
Detail good; negative flat	Over-exposure and under-development	Reduce in potassium ferricyanide reducer; wash; use chromium intensifier
Detail good; negative dense	Over-exposure	Use potassium ferricyanide reducer
Detail good; negative very dense, with shadows fogged	Over-exposure and over-development	Use potassium ferricyanide reducer
Uniform grey fog	Unsafe darkroom light; no restrainer in developer; stale negative material	Generally none; try potassium ferricyanide reducer

Faults in Negatives—continued.

Fault	Cause	Remedy
Coloured fog: greenish on surface, red or violet when looked through	Stale developer; developer contaminated by hypo; stale fixing bath	Use potassium ferricyanide reducer
White spots	Dust in camera; air-bubbles on emulsion during development	Spot with colour to to fill in
Dark spots . .	Undissolved particles of reducing agent in developer	Scrape off, and spot with colour to fill
Streaks showing uneven density	Insufficient agitation during development	None
Running of emulsion, giving distorted image	Drying negative by excessive heat	None
Dark streaks, usually sharply defined	Camera not light-tight	None
Halation: blur of fog around highlights	Unbacked negative material	None
Negative partly positive; fogged	Unsafe darkroom light	None
Reticulation: fine network over negative	Processing solutions at uneven temperatures	None
Scratches	Bad handling or storage of negative	Deep scratch, no real remedy; surface scratch, see below

Scratched negatives: Cover a piece of plain glass on one side with an even layer of glycerine, lower the emulsion side of the negative on to it; and, if the negative is a plate, bind firmly together; if the negative is a film, place another glycerined plain glass on top and bind together. Print by diffused light. Remove, wash and dry negative before storing.

$8 \times 9\frac{1}{2}$
$6\frac{1}{4} \times 9\frac{1}{2}$
$6\frac{1}{2} \times 4\frac{1}{4}$

MAKING PRINTS

WHEN, as a result of previous operations, a suitable negative has been obtained, the next stage is to make a print from it, either by contact (same size) or by projection printing (enlargement).

One rule should be noted here: in all printing processes, at the time of exposure the emulsion side of the negative should always be towards the emulsion side of the printing paper or other material (unless a left-to-right reversal of the image is deliberately intended).

The making of a print follows closely the making of the negative: exposure, development, rinsing, fixing, washing, and drying.

Printing Papers

Papers for making prints are divided into two main groups: contact and enlargement. Enlargement papers are themselves sub-divided into two kinds: bromide and chlorobromide. Nearly all printing papers are made in different grades to suit negatives of varying contrast; and some papers (notably the enlargement type) are made in a variety of surfaces and finishes.

General Characteristics of Papers

Chloride (Contact, "Gaslight"): Silver-chloride emulsion; slow printing; 45–60 sec. development; gives normal blacks; suitable for general printing by contact. Safelight: yellow.

Bromide: Silver-bromide emulsion: fast printing; 2–2½ min. development; gives normal blacks; suitable for general printing by projection. Safelights: orange, green, brown.

Chlorobromide: Mixed silver-bromide and silver-chloride emulsion; medium-fast printing; 2–2½ min. development normally (but see page 98); suitable for printing by projection of portrait, landscape and some other subjects (see table on page 99). Safelights: orange, green brown.

Grades of Papers

Grade	For Printing
Extra Soft	Very contrasty negatives
Soft	Contrasty negatives
Normal	Normal negatives
Hard (Vigorous)	Soft negatives
Extra Hard (Extra Vigorous)	Very soft negatives

Note: Grade should not be confused with surface or finish. Choose grade to suit negative quality; choose surface and finish to suit subject.

Surfaces and Finishes

Bromide and Chlorobromide

Enlarging papers can be obtained in a wide range of surfaces and finishes, some of which are listed below:

Finishes	Surfaces
Glossy	Smooth
Matt	Rough
Semi-matt (Velvet,	Finely Grained
Lustre, Satin)	Grained
	Canvas Grained
Base Colours	Stippled
White	Rayon, etc.
Ivory	
Cream	

Weights
Double
Single
Air Mail

Various combinations of the above qualities can be obtained, for example: Single Weight Velvet Stipple (ivory in colour), Ilford; and Old Master Cream (canvas-grained double weight), Kodak. Makers' lists should be consulted for other combinations.

Contact Papers

These are usually made in Glossy and Semi-matt (smooth white) only.

Printing-paper Sizes

The following sizes, given in inches, correspond closely to the roll-film and plate sizes which are given in inches on pages 56–7. Where paper sizes are also suitable for plates in metric sizes, these are shown in the second and fourth columns.

Paper size	Suitable for metric size	Paper size	Suitable for metric size
(in.)	(cm.)	(in.)	(cm.)
$1\frac{7}{8} \times 2\frac{3}{4}$	$4\cdot5 \times 6$	*$7\frac{1}{8} \times 9\frac{1}{2}$	18×24
$2\frac{1}{4} \times 2\frac{1}{2}$		8×10	
$2\frac{1}{2} \times 3\frac{1}{2}$	6×9	*$9\frac{1}{2} \times 11\frac{3}{4}$	24×30
*$2\frac{1}{4} \times 3\frac{1}{4}$	6×9	10×12	24×30
$2\frac{3}{4} \times 4\frac{1}{2}$		*$11\frac{3}{4} \times 15\frac{3}{4}$	30×40
$3 \times 4\frac{1}{8}$		12×15	
$3\frac{1}{2} \times 4\frac{1}{2}$		15×18	
*$3\frac{1}{2} \times 4\frac{3}{4}$	9×12	16×20	40×50
$3\frac{1}{2} \times 5\frac{1}{2}$		20×24	50×60
4×6	10×15	20×30	
$4\frac{3}{4} \times 6\frac{1}{2}$		24×30	
*$5\frac{1}{8} \times 7\frac{7}{8}$	13×18	24×36	
6×8		30×40	
$6\frac{1}{2} \times 8\frac{1}{2}$			

Special sizes for metric plates.

Artificial Finishes

When enlarging, out-of-the-ordinary finishes can be produced by means of screens. These screens can be placed either in contact with the negative (when they will be enlarged), or at the baseboard in contact or near-contact with the printing paper (when they will appear same-size).

Home-made screens which can be used: muslin, wire-mesh, veiling, net curtaining, glass spattered finely with red ink.

Screens which can be bought: stipple, canvas, tapestry, honeycomb, sand-grain, and some others.

The use of any screen for any particular subject is a matter for individual preference and experiment.

Snow and Rain Screens. Almost any subject (in particular, street scenes and pictorial subjects generally) can be screened artificially to give an effect of snow or rain. The screens are made in the darkroom, as described below.

Sprinkle salt on to matt black paper and make two negatives
(i) with the paper still (for slowly-falling snow); and
(ii) with the paper moved obliquely during exposure (for rain and blizzard effects).

For rain, place screen (ii) in close contact with the negative; for snow, place a thin sheet of glass between the selected screen and negative.

Chlorobromide Tones

Variation of image colour (from warm black through brown to brown-red) can be obtained on chlorobromide papers—usually by increasing exposure, decreasing the strength of the developer, and increasing the development time. Additional potassium bromide is generally added to the developer to counteract the risk of fog during prolonged development.

Each maker has his own formula and instructions for his product, and these should be followed explicitly when tones other than warm black are desired.

Comparative Speeds

If printing conditions were so arranged that a normal print is obtained on bromide paper in 1 sec., then with the same conditions a normal print would be obtained on chlorobromide paper in about $2\frac{1}{2}$ sec. and on contact paper in about 50 sec.

Owing to the very long printing time required, it is impractical to attempt enlargements on contact paper, but bromide or chlorobromide papers could be tried for contact printing (negative and paper being normal) in the following conditions:

Bromide: 4 ft. from 25-watt lamp—4 sec.
Chlorobromide: 4 ft. from 25-watt lamp—10 sec.

Contact Printing Time

With a normal negative, normal paper and a 60-watt pearl lamp without reflector, the following exposures can be tried: 5 sec. at 12 in. from lamp, or 10 sec. at 17 in. from lamp. Thin negatives will require shorter time; dense negatives will require longer; and there will be some variation of exposure when using papers other than normal (slightly shorter for soft grades; slightly longer for contrasty grades).

Enlarging Papers: Suitability for Subject

Subject	Base tint	Surface and finish	Paper
Portraits			
Women . .	Ivory	Smooth or grained; matt or semi-matt	Chlorobromide
Children .	Ivory	Smooth or grained; semi-matt	Chlorobromide
Men . .	White	Smooth; semi-matt	Chlorobromide
Character .	Ivory or cream	Grained or rough; matt	Chlorobromide
Animals . .	White	Smooth; semi-matt	Bromide
Landscape, etc.			
General . .	White or ivory	Rough; matt	Chlorobromide
Cloud . .	White	Smooth; semi-matt	Bromide
Rain . .	White	Smooth; semi-matt	Bromide
Snow . .	White	Smooth; matt	Bromide
Buildings .	White or ivory	Smooth; matt or semi-matt	Bromide
Woods . .	Cream or ivory	Smooth; matt	Chlorobromide
Sunset . .	Cream or ivory	Smooth; semi-matt	Bromide
Night scenes .	White	Smooth; semi-matt	Bromide
Press pictures (all subjects) .	White	Smooth; glossy	Bromide
Interiors . .	White or ivory	Smooth; matt	Bromide
Still life . .	Ivory or cream	Grained; semi-matt	Chlorobromide
Flowers . .	White	Smooth; semi-matt	Bromide

The data in the above table are recommendations only; the paper to be used for any subject is a matter for individual preference and taste.

As regards surfaces, glossy paper must be well glazed if it is to look good; it does not retouch easily, hence negatives for printing on glossy should be free from blemishes. Matt, rough and grained papers can be extensively retouched without unsightliness.

Single-weight paper is best for mounting; double-weight for unmounted framing.

Optical Systems of Enlargers

Recommended optical systems for enlargers, with details of their respective suitabilities, are given below:

Light-source	Condenser	Diffuser	Suitability
Focused point (projection-type lamp)	Double	None	When sharp, contrasty detail is required
Opal or sprayed white lamp*	Double (preferred) or Single	None	General printing
Opal or sprayed white lamp*	Single	Flashed opal	General printing (results slightly softer than above)
Opal or sprayed white lamp*	None	Flashed opal	Retouched portraits; grainy or scratched negatives; for soft results generally

* *Triple-sprayed, not the single-sprayed household variety.*

The Condensers

The diameter of any condenser system should be slightly larger than the diagonal measurement of the largest negative to be printed and usual sizes are:

Negative Size .	24 × 36 mm.	1⅝ × 2¼ in.	2½ × 3½ in.	¼-plate	½-plate	whole-plate
Condenser diameter .	2 in.	3 in.	4½ in.	6 in.	8½ in.	11 in.

Where no condenser is used, the opening through which the light passes from source to negative carrier, and the sheet of flashed opal accompanying it, should be slightly greater than the dimensions of the largest negative to be enlarged.

Enlarger Lens

The rule for an enlarger lens is that it should have a focal length normal for the negative to be used; i.e. it should be the same as, or slightly greater than, the taking lens in the camera.

Where an enlarger is capable of taking negatives of several sizes, then the focal length of the lens should be appropriate for the largest negative to be enlarged. The preceding table for condensers forms a useful guide.

If the focal length of an enlarger lens is less than the diagonal measurement of a negative being enlarged, then

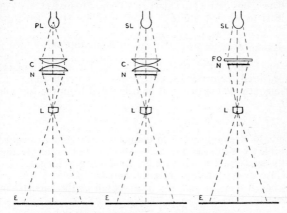

OPTICAL SYSTEMS OF ENLARGERS

1. Point-source of light, PL (to be adjusted at each change of focus), with double condenser C—for maximum definition.

2. Sprayed lamp SL and double condenser C—for general use.

3. Sprayed lamp SL and flashed opal FO—for soft results.

N = negative; L = enlarger lens; E = easel

lighting density over the negative will vary, falling off on those parts of the negative which are in excess of the focal length of the lens.

If the focal length of an enlarger lens is very much greater than the diagonal measurement of a negative being enlarged, the illumination of the negative will be quite satisfactory, but the distance from negative to paper will become great and, for big enlargements, may become beyond the bounds of practicability.

To calculate the height at which an enlarger must work for the maximum enlargement desired, use the formula:

$$D = \frac{F(M+1)^2}{M}$$

where D = distance between negative and paper; F = focal length of lens; M = magnification in diameters desired. All measurements are in inches.

Thus if it is desired to enlarge a VP-size negative ($1\frac{5}{8} \times 2\frac{1}{4}$ in.) at least to whole-plate ($6\frac{1}{2} \times 8\frac{1}{2}$ ins.) with a $4\frac{1}{2}$-in. lens, then

$$D = \frac{4\frac{1}{2}(4+1)^2}{4} = \frac{4\frac{1}{2} \times 25}{4} = 28 \text{ in. approx.}$$

Conversely, if the maximum distance for a given enlarger is measured, the maximum enlargement for any given lens and for any size of negative can be calculated from the formula:

$$M = \frac{D-F}{F}$$

where M = magnification in diameters; D = greatest distance possible from enlarger lens to baseboard; and F = focal length of the enlarger lens. All measurements are in inches.

Thus if the greatest distance possible between lens and baseboard is 36 in. and the focal length of the lens is 3 in., then:

$$M = \frac{36-3}{3} = 11 \text{ diameters}$$

To find the degree of magnification, divide the size of each side of the negative into its corresponding enlargement size; the larger result is the magnification. Thus in the case of enlarging a VP negative to whole-plate, $6\frac{1}{2}$ divided by $1\frac{5}{8} = 4$; and $8\frac{1}{2}$ divided by $2\frac{1}{4} =$ about $3\frac{3}{4}$. Magnification should be taken as 4 diameters.

Magnification and Exposure

In any artificial light system, the intensity of the light varies according to the distance from the light source; that is to say, a light at 2 ft. will give 4 times the intensity of a light at 4ft., but only $\frac{1}{4}$ the intensity of a light at 1 ft.

In enlarger optical systems this rule more or less applies where condensers are not used (i.e. with opal diffusion only).

Where a condenser forms part of the optical system, then the following table will serve as a guide to relative light intensities (and hence to relative exposures) through that system in terms of magnification.

Magnification . (diameters)	2	2½	3	3½	4	4½	5	6	7	8	9	10
Relative exposure .	1	1·4	1·7	2·3	3	3·6	4·2	5·5	7·2	9	11	13·2

To use the above table, multiply the known exposure time by the relative exposure factor for the magnification required, and divide the result by the relative exposure factor for the known exposure time.

For example, supposing the exposure time for enlarging a 24 × 36-mm. (1 × 1½ in.) negative to ¼-plate were 10 sec. and it is desired to make a 10 × 15-in. enlargement from the same negative at the same aperture. What exposure time would be required?

Magnification from negative to ¼-plate may be taken at 3½; magnification from negative to 10 × 15-in. is 10. Therefore the exposure time for the big enlargement would be (approximately):

$$\frac{10 \text{ sec.} \times 13\cdot2}{2\cdot3} = 57 \text{ sec.}$$

Aperture and Exposure

If the aperture of the enlarger lens is altered, the exposure time must be modified roughly in accordance with the table on page 21. Thus, in the above case, if 57 sec. is felt to be too long, and the aperture used was $f.8$, an increase of aperture to $f.4$ would call for only about ¼ the exposure—say 16–17 sec.

Determining Enlargement Exposure

The above methods of determining exposure times must be considered as approximate working guides only. They will not determine any basic exposure time; nor will they produce

any exact exposure time for making a print of the precise
image colour required by the operator.

When printing by projection, the only practical ways of
determining exposure are: (i) by test strip; (ii) by step wedge;
(iii) by enlarger photometer; and (iv) by enlarger photoelectric
meter. The first two use the method of trial exposure; the
last two call for the employment of precision instruments.

Test Strip

To determine exposure by test strip, place the negative in
the enlarger, and adjust and focus for size of print required.
Then place on the baseboard a strip of the printing paper to be
used (about 2×4 in. will do), cover all but $\frac{3}{4}$ in. with black
card, and expose for 5 sec. Uncover a further $\frac{3}{4}$ in. of the
test paper and expose again for 5 sec. Repeat until the whole
of the test paper has been exposed. Now develop and fix
the strip and examine briefly by white light, when the strip
will be found to have steps of varying image densities upon
it, the darkest of these having had the longest exposure time.

Determine which step gives the best image density, and
calculate the exposure by multiplying the number of steps
from the lightest by 5 sec. Thus if the fourth step from
lightest gives the right density, then the exposure time is
20 sec.

For fairly big enlargements, 10 sec. steps might be tried.
When positioning the strip on the baseboard, choose a part
of the negative image which in its range of tones is represen-
tative of the main point of interest of the picture.

Step Wedge

A step wedge is a transparency which is divided into a
number of steps of progressive density, usually ten, from
black to clear white.

To use it, first put a negative in the enlarger and adjust and
focus for the size of print required. Then place on the baseboard a piece of the printing paper to be used and cover it
with the transparency. Expose the whole for a fixed time (say
1 min.), then develop and fix the printing paper. The correct
step on the paper is selected under white light, and the time
of exposure is calculated by multiplying the printing time
for the paper by a factor corresponding to the step selected.

A step wedge can be made and its factors determined by

experiment; alternatively step wedges with accompanying tables can be purchased.

Photometer

This instrument employs the technique of the "disappearing spot," and works as follows: A spot of fixed density is set in the middle of a ring which can be illuminated from beneath by means of a lamp connected to a source of electric current through a variable resistance. The variable resistance is fitted with a pointer which operates over a multiple dial giving details of exposure, aperture and paper speed.

To use, place a negative in the enlarger and adjust for size and focus. Then place the photometer spot under a part of the negative which shows a middle tone, and, watching the spot, vary the light from the ring around it until the spot disappears. The pointer will then give correct exposure for the aperture and paper used.

Photo-electric Meter

This instrument is very similar to the type used for determining negative exposure, except that its sensitivity and dial markings are modified for projection printing. Its method of use is similar to that of a meter calibrated for exposing negatives.

Printing Paper Developers

Notes: Many of the developers, etc., listed below are available already compounded in powder or liquid form—see catalogues. Movement of the print in any developer should be continuous throughout the whole time of development.

All Papers

Kodak D.163—Special Developer

Elon (metol)	.	.	.	20 grains	1·1 grammes
Sodium sulphite (cryst.)	.	3 oz.	37·5 grammes
Hydroquinone	.	.	.	150 grains	8·5 grammes
Sodium carbonate (cryst.)	.	3½ oz.	87·5 grammes
Potassium bromide	.	.	25 grains	1·4 grammes
Water to make	.	.	.	20 oz.	500 c.c.

Dissolve the chemicals in the order given.

Contact paper: Dilute the above with equal parts of water.

Enlarging papers: Dilute the above with 3 parts of water. For somewhat contrasty results on bromide paper, dilute as for contact paper.

Enlarging Papers—Normal Results

Ilford D.20

Metol	. . . .	15 grains	0·75 grammes
Sodium sulphite (cryst.)	.	1 oz.	25 grammes
Hydroquinone	. .	60 grains	3 grammes
Sodium carbonate (cryst.)	.	1½ oz.	40 grammes.
Potassium bromide	.	20 grains	1 gramme
Water to make	. . .	20 oz.	500 c.c.

Dissolve the chemicals in the order given. For use, dilute with 1 part of water.

Enlarging Papers—Soft Results

Kodak D.165

Elon (metol)	. .	52·5 grains	3 gramme
Sodium sulphite (cryst.)	.	1 oz.	25 gramme
Sodium carbonate (cryst.)	.	2 oz.	50 gramme
Potassium bromide	.	9 grains	0·5 gramme
Water to make	. .	20 oz.	500 c.c.

Dissolve the chemicals in the order given. For use, dilute the above with 3 parts water.

Enlarging Papers—Contrasty Results

Kodak D.72

Elon (metol)	. .	27·5 grains	1·55 gramme
Sodium sulphite (cryst.)	.	1 oz. 350 gr.	45 gramme
Hydroquinone	. .	105 grains	6 gramme
Sodium carbonate (cryst.)	.	3 oz. 262 gr.	90 gramm
Potassium bromide	.	16·25 grains	0·95 gramme
Water to make	. . .	20 oz.	500 c.c.

Dissolve the chemicals in the order given. For use, dilute with 1 part of water.

All Papers—for Pure Blacks

Sodium sulphite (cryst.)	.	1 oz.	27·5 grammes
Potassium bromide	.	12 grains	0·8 grammes
Water to make	. .	20 oz.	500 c.c.

and immediately before use, add

Amidol	. . .	48 grains	2·75 grammes

Notes: This developer does not keep. For contact papers the potassium bromide should be reduced to 3 grains (0·2 grammes).

Stop Bath

Potassium metabisulphite	.	½ oz.	12½ grammes
Water	. . .	20 oz.	500 c.c.

or

Acetic acid (glacial)	. .	20 minims	1¼ c.c.
Water	. . .	20 oz.	500 c.c.

The time prints should be in a stop bath is at least 10 sec.; movement of the print in the bath should be continuous.

Fixing Baths

The basis of all fixing baths for prints is a 20% solution of hypo (sodium thiosulphate). This is somewhat weaker than that used for fixing negative material.

There are three fixing baths, as follows: plain (not much used now); acid fix (the standard fixing bath, for use when the prints are to be dried without heat); and acid fix with hardener (for use when the prints are to be heat-dried).

Plain Fix

Hypo	. . . .	4 oz.	100 grammes
Water	. . . .	20 oz.	500 c.c.

Acid Fix

Hypo	. . . .	4 oz.	100 grammes
Potassium metabisulphite	.	½ oz.	12½ grammes
Water	. . . .	20 oz.	500 c.c.

Acid Fix with Hardener

Hypo	.	.	.	4 oz.	100 gramme
Potassium metabisulphite	.	$\frac{1}{2}$ oz.	$12\frac{1}{2}$ gramme
Chrome alum	.	.	$\frac{1}{2}$ oz.	$12\frac{1}{2}$ gramme
Water	.	.	.	20 oz.	500 c.c.

The time prints should be in any fixing bath (at 65°F.) at least 10 min. Movement of the print should be continuou for the first $\frac{1}{2}$ min.; thereafter it can be occasional.

After-treatment of Prints

Sepia Toning

Two solutions are needed: 1, bleaching bath; and 2, tonir bath.

1. Potassium ferricyanide	.	1 oz.	25 gramme
Potassium bromide.	.	1 oz.	25 gramm
Water to make	.	.	20 oz.	500 c.c.
2. Sodium sulphide	.	.	87·5 grains	5 gramm
Water to make	.	.	20 oz.	500 c.c.

(*Note:* Solution 2 does not keep. To obtain the best sepi new solution should be used for each print. Solution 1 ca be used repeatedly until it no longer bleaches.)

To use, bleach the print in solution 1 until the last blacl have gone, wash until all yellow coloration has cleared (lea ing the image light brown), then immerse in solution 2 for few minutes. Finally wash for 5 min.

It should be noted that negatives can be sepia toned described above in order to give them greater permanen and—in the case of slightly thin negatives—better printi quality.

Intensification

Prints on bromide which are flat and slightly lacking contrast can sometimes be improved by bleaching in subdu light with the chromium bleach given on page 91, washi thoroughly, and redeveloping in strong light (not direct su light) in a suitable developer.

Reduction

Prints which are too contrasty or are fogged may be reduc or cleared in the Farmer's reducer given on page 92. Prir

The specimen record arrangement shown below should be ruled across two pages of a quarto (8 × 10 in.) book, which should have an A–Z index in front.

When using the book, particular note should be made in the Remarks column of any filter used, any after-treatment given to negative or print, and any "holding back" or prolonged exposure.

PRINT / NEG

Subject	No.	Paper	Grade	Magnification	Stop	Exp.	No.	Negative Material	Focus

ATIVE

Lighting	Stop	Exp.	Developer	Temp.	Time	Remarks

which have been over-exposed during enlarging may be reduced generally in the following special print reducers:

Iodine-Cyanide Reducer (Ilford Formula)

Two solutions are required:

1. Potassium iodide	.	.	$\frac{1}{4}$ oz.	6 grammes
Iodine	.	.	20 grains	1 gramme
Water to make	.	.	10 oz.	250 c.c.
2. Potassium cyanide	.	.	40 grains	2 grammes
Water to make	.	.	10 oz.	250 c.c.

(*Note that potassium cyanide is a particularly deadly poison, and must be used with extreme care.*)

For use, take 1 oz. (25 c.c.) of each solution, mix, and add water to make 20 oz. (500 c.c.).

Permanganate Reducer

Potassium permanganate	.	5 grains	0·25 grammes
Sulphuric acid (conc.)	.	45 minims	2·5 grammes
Water to make	.	.	20 oz.	500 c.c.

For use, dilute the above with 2 parts of water. This reducer works very slowly.

When reducing by either of the above formulæ, reduction may be stopped at any point by washing quickly in plain water. The final wash should be for 10 min.

Yellow Stains

Yellow stains left in prints as a result of processing may be removed by immersion for a few minutes in the following bath:

Alum	.	.	.	$1\frac{1}{4}$ oz.	31·25 gramme
Hydrochloric acid (conc.)	.	$\frac{1}{2}$ oz.	12 c.c.
Water to make	.	.	20 oz.	500 c.c.

Faults in Prints

Where the negative from which any print is made is normal it is recommended that any faulty print be scrapped and a good print made. Where the negative has small errors in contrast, acceptable prints will result from using a suitable grade of paper (see page 96). If the negative is not normal, see page 93.

Fault	Cause	Remedy
Contrast good; print too light	Under-exposure, or insufficient development	None; reprint
Contrast good; print too dark	Over-exposure	None; reprint
Contrast poor; print looks dull	Over-exposure and under-development *or*	Try chromium intensifier
	Paper too soft for negative	None; reprint on harder paper
Contrast poor; print looks hard	Paper too hard for negative	Reprint on softer paper, or try reduction
General grey fog .	Unsafe darkroom light	Try reduction in iodine-cyanide
Uneven density .	Developer exhausted; or no movement in fixing bath for first 10 sec.	None; reprint
White spots . .	Dust on negative or paper during printing	Spot with colour to fill
Muddy blacks. .	Exhausted developer; or too much bromide in developer	None; reprint
Poor blacks; greyish whites	Too much bromide in developer	None; reprint
Mottled whites .	Prolonged development or stale paper	None: reprint
Yellowish whites .	As for mottled whites; or developer contaminated by hypo	None; reprint
Blisters . . .	Processing solutions at widely differing temperatures; or too strong a fixing solution; or too much alkali in developer	None; reprint
Prints turn yellow in storage	Insufficient fixing or washing; impure mounting paste	None; reprint

Faults in Prints (continued).

Fault	Cause	Remedy
Image reversed right to left	Negative emulsion away from instead of towards paper during printing	None; reprint
Scum on print. .	Hard water used for processing	Immerse in 1% hydrochloric acid solution
Print out of focus (negative good)	Contact: negative and paper not in contact when printing	None; reprint
	Enlargement: enlarger lens not properly focused	None; reprint
Print lacks definition (negative good)	Enlarger lens dusty or otherwise unclean	None: reprint

MISCELLANEOUS DARKROOM NOTES

Cleansing Dishes

Dishes and tanks can be cleaned effectively with either of the two following solutions:

1.	Hydrochloric acid (conc.)	4 oz.	100 c.c.
	Water	20 oz.	500 c.c.
2.	Potassium bichromate .	$1\frac{3}{4}$ oz.	45 gramme
	Sulphuric acid (conc.) .	2 oz.	50 gramme
	Water	20 oz.	500 c.c.

(*Important note: Add acid little by little to water, never water to acid.*)

Dishes or tanks to be cleaned should be acted upon by either of the above cleansers for about 1 min., then washed very thoroughly in running water.

Crystalline and Anhydrous Salts

In formulæ throughout this book, the quantities of sodium salts are given for their crystalline forms. If the anhydrous forms are used, the following particulars should be noted and the formulæ adjusted accordingly:

Sodium sulphite: 1 part anhydrous = 2 parts crystalline
Sodium carbonate: 3 parts anhydrous = 8 parts crystalline

Weights and Measures

Imperial

Avoirdupois

437½ grains =	1 ounce (oz.)
7000 grains = 16 ounces =	1 pound (lb.)

Volume

60 minims =	1 drachm
8 drachms = 480 minims =	1 fluid ounce
20 fluid ounces =	1 pint

(*Note that the U.S. pint = 16 U.S. fluid ounces = about 16·5 Imperial fluid ounces. The U.S. grain and the Imperial grain are the same.*)

Useful Equivalents

1 minim = 0·91 grain =	0·059 c.c.
1 grain =	0·065 gramme
1 ounce = 28·35 grammes =	28·42 c.c.
1 pound =	453·59 grammes
1 pint =	568·34 c.c.
1 gramme =	15·4 grains
1 kilogramme = 1000 grammes =	2·2046 pounds
1 cubic centimetre (c.c.) =	16·9 minims
500 cubic centimetres = 0·88 pint =	17·61 ounces

(*Note that 1 fluid ounce = 1 ounce avoir. = 437½ grains = 480 minims.*)

Life of Solutions

The area of sensitive material which can be processed by 20 oz. of average developer is about 400 sq. in. for negative material and about 600 sq. in. for prints.

In the table overleaf are given the numbers of plates (or cut films) and the numbers of prints of various sizes which can be processed safely in 20 oz. of working solutions.

Many experienced workers recommend that not more than 5 roll films be developed in any developer at dish strength or more than 3 roll films in any developer at tank strength. Development time should be increased by about 5% for successive films in the former case, and by about 10% in the latter case (e.g. if the time for the first film is 10 min. at 65°F., then the time for the second film would be about 11 min. and the time for the third about 12 min. at the same temperature for tank-strength development).

When developing plates and cut films, slight increases of time should be allowed for each half-dozen pieces processed (or for each piece of the larger sizes) after the first.

Size of material*	Developer		Stop bath		Acid fix	
	Plates	Prints	Plates	Prints	Plates	Prints
2×2† . . .	90		54		200	
$3\frac{1}{4} \times 3\frac{1}{4}$† . .	35		20		80	
$2\frac{1}{4} \times 2\frac{1}{4}$ . . .		110		65		260
$3\frac{1}{2} \times 2\frac{1}{2}$ . . .	40	80	24	48	100	200
$\frac{1}{4}$-plate . . .	24	48	15	30	60	120
Postcard . . .	18	36	10	20	40	80
$\frac{1}{2}$-plate . . .	12	24	7	14	30	60
Whole-plate . .	6	12	3	7	12	25
10×8 . . .	4	8	2	5	8	18
12×10 . . .	2	5	1	3	4	10
15×12 . . .	1	2	1‡	1	2	4

* *Plates or cut films (for roll film, see notes above table).*
† *Lantern plates.*   ‡ *Per 40 oz. working solution.*

Notes on Photo Chemicals

Acetic acid, glacial, is used principally for making stop baths and occasionally in fixing baths to make them acid.

Amidol (di-aminophenol hydrochloride), a reducing agent for developers—very poor keeping qualities when in solution. Used principally for the production of good blacks in prints, occasionally for the development of negatives.

Ammonium persulphate, an agent for the reduction of contrast in negatives.

Borax, a mild alkali used as the accelerator (whole or part) in fine-grain developers.

Caustic soda (sodium hydroxide), a powerful alkali used generally for the accelerator bath of two-bath developers.

Chrome alum (potassium chrome alum or ammonium chrome alum) is used as a hardener for negatives and prints, both for processing in tropical conditions and for occasions when drying is to be by heat:

Citric acid, occasionally used as a substitute for acetic acid.

Elon, a Kodak proprietary brand of metol.

Glycin (para-hydroxyphenyl glycin), a very gentle reducing agent used in ultra-fine-grain developers.

Hydrochloric acid is mostly used in the bleaching bath that precedes redevelopment when intensifying negatives; it can also be used in weak solution for the cleansing of dishes, tanks, etc., and for the removal of hard-water scum from negatives and prints.

Hydroquinone (quinol, or para-hydroxybenzene), a reducing agent for developers which gives high contrast.

Hypo (sodium thiosulphate), the standard fixing agent; also used in an after-treatment process for clearing fog and reducing density in negatives and, occasionally, prints.

Meritol, a Johnson proprietary reducing agent for very fine-grain developers.

Metol (monomethyl para-aminophenol sulphate), a reducing agent for developers which gives soft contrast and great detail. It is frequently used with hydroquinone (which has somewhat opposite qualities) in well-balanced developers for all types of negative material which do not call for exceptionally fine-grain, and for positive material.

(*Note: This chemical is poisonous to a few people, setting up a painful irritation of the skin. In such cases, the use of rubber gloves when processing is the only real preventative. Most people are not affected.*)

Para-phenylene diamine, a very gentle reducing agent used in ultra-fine-grain developers, either as the sole reducer or in combination with glycin and/or metol. (*See Note below Metol.*)

Potassium bichromate, used with hydrochloric acid in the bleaching bath that precedes redevelopment when intensifying negatives.

Potassium bromide, used as the restrainer in practically all developers except ultra-fine-grain and two-bath.

Potassium cyanide, one of the constituents in the iodine-cyanide treatment of prints whose highlights have become fogged. (*Note: this chemical is highly poisonous.*)

Potassium ferricyanide, used in conjunction with hypo as a reducer of density in negatives and, to some extent, prints.

Potassium iodide, used in conjunction with potassium cyanide for the after-treatment of prints; used also as a restrainer with potassium bromide in some developers.

Potassium metabisulphite, one of the preservatives used in developers, also used in fixing baths to make them acid.

Pyro (pyrogallic acid, trihydroxybenzene), a reducing agent for developers with somewhat poor keeping qualities when in solution. It is vigorous and gives good gradation, but because it readily oxidises and deposits a brown stain on negatives it tends to give contrasty prints—for that reason it is considered valuable in cases of under-exposure.

Sodium bisulphite, a preservative used in some developers.

Sodium carbonate (anhydrous or crystalline), the commonest of the accelerators used in developers generally.

Sodium sulphite (anhydrous or crystalline), the principal preservative used in developers generally.

Sulphuric acid, used in conjunction with ammonium persulphate in the after-treatment of negatives which are dense and contrasty through over-development.

Uranium nitrate, used in conjunction with potassium ferricyanide for the quick intensification of negatives which have been under-exposed.

Part Four

LANTERN SLIDES

APPARATUS

First Considerations

THE essential difference between lantern photography and print photography is that the final result is to be viewed by projection through a transparency (a lantern slide) and not by reflected light from a paper base (a print). The process of making lantern slides up to the negative stage is exactly the same as for making prints in black-and-white photography; in colour photography the usual rule is to produce a transparency in any event.

The production of a black-and-white positive transparency is similar to the production of a print inasmuch that printing is either by contact or by enlargement, but on plate or film instead of on paper. Once made, the transparency usually has to be prepared for use in a lantern as described later.

The apparatus used for production of the negative is precisely the same as for general photography, and all the considerations of selection of camera, lens, shutter and accessories apply. It is immaterial whether the negative is made on film or plate.

A few cameras are still available—mainly secondhand—which will produce standard lantern slides for printing by contact, but the tendency nowadays is to produce a negative with ordinary equipment and to make the slide by enlargement if the negative is small, by contact from the whole negative if it is of suitable size, or from a selected part if it is large; or by reduction if the whole of a large negative is to appear on the slide.

117

Transparency Projectors

The apparatus for projecting lantern slides is made in three sizes: miniature (2-in. square slides), standard ($3\frac{1}{4}$-in. square slides), and film strip (24×36-mm. frames on 36-mm. ciné film).

Miniature. This size, because of its portability and the wide use of 35-mm. cameras, is tending to take the place of the standard ($3\frac{1}{4}$-in.) size, except for lecture purposes in large halls. The slide carrier takes slides of 2×2 in., of metal or glass, mostly with cut-outs for 24×36-mm. positives. As an example of portability, a projector of this size is made which fits into a small carrying case that provides room for 50 slides and a small rigid screen.

Standard. This size is, as has already been indicated, suitable for large halls. The slide carrier will take slides of $3\frac{1}{4} \times 3\frac{1}{4}$ in. and can be readily adapted to take the 2×2-in. size.

Film Strip. This type of projector does not, as a rule, have a slide carrier, but a "gate" and pressure springs for positioning and holding individual pictures contained on a continuous 35-mm. film of ciné type, and two bobbins on to which the film is wound. It may take from 50 to 100 pictures on a single film, each one of which may be projected in order by the simple turning of a handle.

Combination Projectors

Apparatus may be had which will take both individual slides and film strip. The most versatile of these is the standard-size projector which will take $3\frac{1}{4} \times 3\frac{1}{4}$-in. slides, plus 2×2-in. with a carrier adaptor, plus film strip by fitting film strip holders. Further, projectors of the slide-carrier type can be fitted with an adaptor for the projection of microscope slides.

Episcopes. These instruments, although not made for the projection of lantern slides, are mentioned here as part of the means of projecting photographs. They project not by direct light through a transparency, but by reflected light from prints; they will also project from other opaque objects such as printed pages, maps, coins, etc. They are of interest to the photographer who prefers to project his pictures because they can be had in combination with transparency projectors, when they are known as "epidiascopes."

Screens

While some projectionists are content to throw their pictures on to a whitewashed or lightly colour-washed wall (and this method is often suitable in the home if the wall is of good surface and if only monochrome pictures are being projected), a projection screen always gives superior results.

A household sheet or tablecloth is not generally suitable for such a screen because the essence of a good screen is its ability to reflect the light thrown upon it, and domestic fabrics pass a great deal of light through themselves, this light being lost to the viewer, giving him the impression of a dull picture.

Manufactured screens are of two principal types: (i) the flat, matt-finished screen which gives a high degree of reflectivity and offers comfortable viewing to persons sitting well to the side of the line of projection throw; and (ii) the crystal screen, the surface of which is set with a great number of minute crystal beads mounted to give the greatest possible reflectivity, offering extremely bright pictures to persons sitting close to the line of projection throw. Both types of screen are made to roll up into small compass when not in use.

Picture Size

The size of the picture which is projected depends upon three factors: (i) the focal length of the projection lens; (ii) the length of throw (i.e. the distance between lens and screen); and (iii) the size or pattern of the projector lamp-house and strength of the projector lamp.

Concerning this last point, a good picture must have a fair degree of brightness, calling for a high-power projector lamp. But such lamps by their nature generate considerable heat, and will do damage on continuous burning unless the lamp-house is either large enough or is fitted with some means of artificial ventilation to dissipate the heat safely. Projection lamps of many powers may be bought to work on a variety of voltages (mains or battery); they are sometimes silvered for reflection. The best lamp to use is advised by the makers of the projector.

Adequate brightness being assumed, picture size may be regulated by selection of lens and adjustment of throw, as shown in the following tables. In these tables, the figures, etc., under "Size of projected picture" relate to the focal length of the lenses used. Dimension of picture is approximate for longest side.

Throw (ft.)	Miniature frame (2 in. sq.)				Standard frame (3¼ in. sq.)			
	Size of projected picture				Size of projected picture			
	4 in.	6 in.	8 in.	12 in.	4 in.	6 in.	8 in.	12in.
	ft. in.	ft. in.	ft. in.	ft. in.	ft. in.	ft. in.	ft. in.	ft. in.
6	2 5	1 8	1 3	—	4 3	2 8	2 1	1 5
8	3 2	2 2	1 8	—	5 8	3 9	2 8	1 9
10	4 0	2 7	2 0	1 5	7 0	4 8	3 6	2 2
12	4 9	3 2	2 4	1 7	8 3	5 5	4 1	2 9
15	5 9	4 0	3 0	2 0	10 3	6 9	5 2	3 6
20	7 9	5 6	3 9	2 5	13 6	7 9	7 0	4 6
30	12 3	8 0	6 0	4 0	21 6	14 6	10 6	7 0
40	16 9	11 3	8 0	5 9	—	19 0	14 6	9 0
50	21 0	13 9	10 3	6 9	—	23 6	17 6	11 6

Throw (ft.)	Frame = 24 × 36 mm.			
	Size of projected picture			
	2 in.	3 in.	4 in.	6 in.
	ft. in.	ft. in.	ft. in.	ft. in.
6	4 4	2 10	2 2	1 5
8	5 8	3 9	2 9	1 10
10	7 0	4 9	3 5	2 4
12	8 3	5 6	4 2	2 9
15	10 0	6 8	5 0	3 6
20	14 0	9 6	7 0	4 6
30	21 6	14 0	10 6	7 0
40	—	19 0	14 0	9 6
50	—	23 6	18 0	11 9

Note: Blanks in the tables opposite indicate that the picture would be impracticably large or small, and that a lens of more suitable focal length should be used.

To work out size of picture from any focal length, the following formula may be used:

$$P = \frac{d-F}{F} \times S$$

where P = size of largest dimension of picture on screen; d = distance between lens and screen (i.e. "throw"); F = focal length of lens; and S = size of largest dimension of picture on slide to be projected.

MAKING POSITIVE TRANSPARENCIES

THE negative having been obtained by normal methods, the making of slides is a matter of printing a positive on glass or film, and mounting the result in such a way that it is suitable for passing through the projector. On the whole it is more convenient to make the positive on glass—subsequent mounting will be rather easier.

Lantern Plates

Lantern plates can be obtained suitable either for enlarging or for contact printing. Rich blacks can be obtained on plates with a bromide emulsion, and may be converted to sepia by the normal sepia toning process. Warm black and browns can be obtained on plates with a chlorobromide emulsion. Ordinary black will be given by contact slides with a chloride emulsion (for comparisons, see Printing Papers, page 95). The speeds of printing are roughly the same as for bromide, chlorobromide and chloride papers, and the safelights to be used in the darkroom are the same.

Processing, too, is the same. Good results will be given with any developer appropriate to the paper and the degree of contrast required, and reference should be made to the relevant sections of this book. Manufacturers of lantern plates have special formulæ; on the whole these formulæ are of the metol-hydroquinone type, and any good similar developer may be used.

After development, lantern plates should be rinsed, fixed, washed and dried in the usual way.

Film Strip

The usual size of negative for film strip is 24×36-mm., taken on standard 35-mm. ciné-type film, and these negatives may be used in two ways: (i) separately, mounted into 2-in. square plate holders for miniature lanterns; or (ii) in continuous strips for use in film-strip projectors.

In both cases positives have to be made from the negative strips, and because of the size of the negative and the great degree of accuracy required, the work is best done by a processing firm specialising in such work. The mounting of separate positives into 2-in. slides or the editing of pictures into sequences may be done under home conditions, the former in the way described below and the latter in the way described for the editing of sub-standard ciné film (see page 133.)

Mounting

The following materials will be required for mounting positives as lantern slides:

Cover glasses (2×2 in. or $3\frac{1}{4} \times 3\frac{1}{4}$ in.), or *Frames* (2×2 in., in metal or plastic, cut out for 24×36-mm. positives).

Black paper for masking.

Binding strips for binding.

Film cement, if positives are on film.

White ink and pen for marking directly on to masking paper (alternatively, white gummed paper and black ink may be used).

White gummed paper for spotting (and possibly for marking; see above).

Set-square, cutting knife and steel rule for making masks.

Dusting brush, 1 in., very soft.

For making a slide, first examine the positive and decide upon the exact area of the picture to be used. Then make a mask of black paper, the outer dimensions to be either 2 in. or $3\frac{1}{4}$ in. square according to the size of the cover glasses, the inner dimensions to be according to the picture area selected. If the positive is on glass, place it emulsion-side upwards, put the mask over it, mark and spot the mask as described below, cover the whole with a cover glass and bind up squarely and securely.

If the positive is on film, first put down a cover glass, then on to it place the positive emulsion-side upwards; place over this the mask, carefully position the positive under the mask, and secure the positive to the cover glass with a spot or two of film cement. Finally, mark and spot the mask, put a second cover glass over, and bind the whole squarely.

Important Notes: During the assembling of the slide, keep the dusting brush constantly in use. Before finally binding up, warm cover glasses, positive and mask by gentle heat to drive off all moisture.

Marking and Spotting. The mask should be marked with the title or other description of the picture, preferably underneath the picture as seen when held up to the light. Then,

MAKING
LANTERN
SLIDES

The larger diagram is of a 3¼-in. slide marked in the double-spot system; the smaller is of a 2-in. slide marked in the RPS-approved system—both half size. Apart from spotting, slides should also be marked (not for projection) with a subject-and-number label to facilitate handling

in each of the two top corners place a small spot of white gummed paper. The markings and spotting should be visible through the top cover glass when the slide is bound up, the final appearance being as shown here.

An alternative method of spotting, approved by the Royal

Photographic Society, is to place only one spot at the bottom left-hand corner.

For projection, the slide is placed in the slide-carrier so that with the two-spot method of marking, the spots are at the bottom when facing the projector lamp; and with the one-spot method, the spot is at the top right-hand corner when facing the projector lamp.

Faults in Slides

Faults likely to occur in lantern slides are, so far as negatives and positives are concerned, similar to the faults found in negatives and prints in ordinary photography, and may be remedied in the same ways—by intensification, reduction, etc. Faults peculiar to slides are unsquare mounting, and dust and moisture trapped within the glasses; none of these should appear if reasonable care is exercised on the mounting bench.

Part Five

SUB-STANDARD CINÉ

SUB-STANDARD FILM

Sizes

STANDARD-SIZE cinematograph film is 35 mm. wide, and it is this width which is used in the 35-mm. precision cameras of the Leica type.

This size would be too bulky and too expensive for non-professional cinematography, however, and smaller sizes are produced which have the general name "sub-standard ciné."

There are three sub-standard sizes: 16 mm., 9·5 mm. and 8 mm. Details of these sizes are summarised in the table below, and in the diagrams overleaf.

Width	Silent		Sound		Relative cost*
	Size of frame (mm.)	Frames per ft.	Size of frame (mm.)	Frames per ft.	
16 mm. .	10·41 × 7·47	40	10·41 × 7·47	40	13s. (B) 17s. (C)
9·5 mm. .	8·8 × 7·0	40	6·85 × 5·87	40	11s. (B) No colour
8 mm. .	4·8 × 3·51	80	No sound		5s. (B) 8s. (C)

* *Approximate per-minute projection time (1953): B = Black-and-white; C = Colour.*

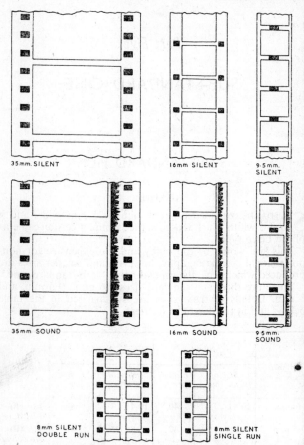

35mm. SILENT   16mm SILENT   9·5 mm. SILENT

35mm SOUND   16mm SOUND   9·5 mm. SOUND

8mm SILENT DOUBLE RUN   8mm SILENT SINGLE RUN

CINÉ-FILM SIZES

Above are actual sizes of standard and sub-standard ciné film, showing (in black) the placement of perforations and sound tracks. Note the differences in perforation of 16 mm. and double-8 mm.

From the foregoing it will be observed that sound is not available on 8 mm. and colour is not available on 9·5 mm.

The 8-mm. size can be purchased in two ways, according to the camera being used: either as 8 mm. or as 16 mm. which can be exposed in the camera twice and split down the middle after processing. The sizes are referred to as "Single 8" and "Double 8" respectively, and it should be noted that Double 8 is not the same as the ordinary 16-mm. stock—the perforations are different.

Film Stock

All sub-standard film stock in current use is panchromatic, and comes in two forms: negative and reversal.

Negative operates in the same way as ordinary negative material in black-and-white photography (i.e. it produces a negative from which positive prints are made), and is most generally used where serious sub-standard film production is contemplated, for it will give positives for editing and, after the negative is matched to the edited positive, projection-positives which are without joins.

Reversal stock (in which is included all presently available colour without special order) is for use where only one copy is required, the film actually passed through the camera being processed into a positive for operation in the projector.

Sub-standard stock follows much the same principles as still photography material: it can be bought in various speeds, the general rule being—the higher the speed, the coarser the grain.

The table overleaf gives a list of some of the better-known sub-standard stock which is available at the time of going to press.

EXPOSURE

IF cinematography is regarded as the taking of a number of still pictures in rapid and regular succession, it will be apparent that the principles of taking still pictures apply equally to cinematography. This is so in all matters relating to focal lengths of lenses, lens apertures, depth of field, shutter-speed and so on, and reference to the appropriate sections of this

List of Ciné Film Stock

Width	Description	Type	Speed (°Sch.)		Packings*
			D	A	
16 mm.	Gevaert Micropan	Reversal	23	21	50, 100
	Panchromosa	Negative	27	25	50, 100
	Superpan	Reversal	27	25	50, 100
	Ultrapan	Reversal	32	31	50, 100
	Ilford HP3	Negative	32	30	50, 100
	Pan F	Negative	25	23	50, 100
	Kodak Plus X	Negative	29	26	100, 200
	Super X	Reversal	28	27	50, 100
	Super XX	Negative and Reversal	32	31	50, 100
	Kodachrome A	Reversal	—	22	50, 100
	D	Reversal	21	—	50, 100
9·5 mm.	Gevaert Micropan	Reversal	23	21	30, 50, 100
	Panchromosa	Negative	27	25	30, 50, 100
	Superpan	Reversal	27	25	30, 50, 100
	Ultrapan	Reversal	32	31	30, 50, 100
	Pathé SS Pan	Reversal	26	24	30, 50
	Super Pan	Reversal	32	31	30, 50
8 mm.	Gevaert Micropan	Reversal	23	21	33 (S), 25, 50, 100 (D)
	Superpan	Reversal	27	25	do.
	Kodak Panchromatic	Reversal	22	20	25 (D)
	Super X	Reversal	28	27	25 (D)
	Kodachrome A	Reversal	—	22	25 (D)
	D	Reversal	21	—	25 (D)

Length in feet. Under "Speed": D=Daylight; A=Artificial Light (Photoflood 3400°K.). Under "Packings": S=Single 8; D=Double 8 (16-mm. stock with 8-mm. perforations, to be split in processing).

book will give certain data respecting them. Further data of use almost entirely to cinematographers are to be found below.

Camera Speeds

For normal taking (and subsequent normal projection), the speed with which sub-standard ciné film passes through the camera is such that individual pictures (frames) are exposed at the following speeds: silent film, 16 per second; sound film, 24 per second. If, the individual frames having been taken at these speeds, they are eventually projected at the same speeds, the rate of movement on the screen will be the same as the rate of movement of the subject photographed.

The frames are exposed in the camera by an intermittent action as follows: light is shut off from the film by a shutter, and the film is moved past the lens in readiness to expose a frame; the film stops moving, and the shutter opens, admitting light through the lens to the film; the shutter closes and the film is automatically moved in readiness for the exposure of the next frame; the cycle of actions is repeated continuously, at the rate of 16 or 24 per second.

During the cycle the shutter is open for exposure for about one-half the time of the complete cycle. Hence, if the rate is 16 frames per second, the shutter-speed for the exposure of each individual frame is reckoned as $\frac{1}{32}$ sec. and if the rate is 24 per second, the shutter-speed is reckoned as $\frac{1}{50}$ sec. These shutter-speeds apply to all normal rate cinematography. They are fixed, and variations of exposure to meet varying light conditions are made entirely by adjustment of lens aperture.

Fast and Slow Motion

The usual practice in all cinematography is to project films at a set speed: 16 frames per second for silent and 24 frames per second for sound. Fast- and slow-motion effects are achieved by varying the speed of taking the film in the camera.

For fast motion, the camera is set to run slow (say at 8 frames per second for silent). For slow-motion, the camera is set to run fast (say 32 frames per second). Altering the speed at which the camera runs affects the shutter-speed in proportion. Thus at 8 frames per second, the shutter-speed is reckoned at $\frac{1}{16}$ sec.; at 32 frames per second, the shutter-speed is $\frac{1}{64}$ sec. These changes must be taken into account when working out lens aperture for correct exposure.

Film Expenditure

Most cinematographers consider that the average shot of any scene or sequence of movement does not exceed 10 sec., and this figure should be kept in mind when the shooting of

9

any scene is contemplated and the reel of film left unexposed in the camera is nearing its end.

The table on page 138 acts as a guide to footage of film used during operation of the camera. It is also a guide (in its higher numbers) to the time any length of film will run through the projector at 16 or 24 frames per second.

Raw film in packings of standard lengths will run in the camera at normal speed for the following times (roughly) in minutes:

Feet	16 and 9·5 mm.		8 mm. Silent
	Silent	Sound	
25			2
30	$1\frac{1}{4}$	$\frac{3}{4}$	
33			$2\frac{1}{2}$
50	2	$1\frac{1}{4}$	4
100	4	$2\frac{3}{4}$	8
200	8	$5\frac{1}{2}$	

Focal Lengths

The usual lenses fitted to or used with sub-standard cine cameras are:

Size	Standard	For Close-up	For Distance
16 mm. .	25 mm. (1 in.)	15 mm. ($\frac{5}{8}$ in.)	50 mm. or 75 mm. (2 in. or 3 in.)
9·5 mm. .	20 mm. ($\frac{3}{4}$ in.)	$12\frac{1}{2}$ mm. ($\frac{1}{2}$ in.)	40 mm. or 60 mm. ($1\frac{1}{2}$ in. or $2\frac{3}{8}$ in.)
8 mm. .	$12\frac{1}{2}$ mm. ($\frac{1}{2}$ in.)	7 mm. ($\frac{1}{4}$ in.)	25 mm. or 40 mm. (1 in. or $1\frac{1}{2}$ in.)

It will be noted that the focal lengths of the lenses are shown primarily in millimetres. The inch-equivalents are approximate.

Depth of Field

The shortness of the focal lengths of most sub-standard ciné lenses is such that depth of field is very large. On the other hand the degree of magnification of the image as projected on to the screen is also large; hence it is usual in all sub-standard ciné work to base all focus on a circle of confusion of $\frac{1}{1000}$ in. or better (see pages 21 to 23).

Below are tables showing the hyperfocal lengths of standard ciné lenses and depths of field. Data for lenses not shown may be calculated from the formulæ shown on page 23.

Hyperfocal Distances

Focal length of lens (mm.)	Stop							
	1·4	1·9	2·8	4·8	5·6	8	11	16
12½	14·9	10·6	7·2	5·0	3·6	2·5	1·8	1·3
20	38·0	27·2	18·5	12·9	9·4	6·9	4·7	3·7
25	58·0	42·5	28·8	20·2	14·4	10·1	7·3	5·4

The distances in the above table are in feet. Depth of Field Tables will be found on pages 139–140.

Exposure Notes

As in still photography, exposure may be determined by tables, calculators or meters, it being remembered that shutter-speed is constant ($\frac{1}{32}$ sec. for silent pictures at normal running), and that exposure is regulated by lens aperture (or stop).

If for slow-motion pictures the running of the camera is set to twice normal (shutter-speed $\frac{1}{64}$ sec.), the lens aperture is enlarged by one whole stop.

If for fast-motion pictures the running of the camera is set to half normal (shutter-speed $\frac{1}{16}$ sec.), the lens aperture is made smaller by one whole stop.

Adjustments to exposure must also be made for film speed (page 128), any filter used (page 37), and subject (page 61).

As rough guides to exposure in the absence of a calculator or meter, the tables overleaf will, if used correctly, give acceptable results.

Exposure Tables

Daylight

Month, and time of day (GMT)	Full sun white cloud	Full sun blue sky	Hazy sun	Dull	Very dull
May to Aug					
10 a.m. to 3 p.m.	f. 16	f. 11	f. 8	f. 5·6	f. 4
8–10 or 3–6 .	f. 11	f. 8	f. 5·6	f. 4	f. 2·8
7–8 or 6–7 .	f. 8	f. 5·6	f. 4	f. 2·8	f. 1·9
Sept., Oct., Mar., or April					
10 a.m. to 3 p.m.	f. 11	f. 8	f. 5·6	f. 4	f. 2·8
8—10 or 3–5 .	f. 8	f. 5·6	f. 4	f. 2·8	f. 1·9
Nov. to Feb.					
10 a.m. to 3 p.m.	f. 8	f. 5·6	f. 4	f. 2·8	f. 1·9
9–10 or 3–4 .	f. 5·6	f. 4	f. 2·8	f. 1·9	f. 1·4

Film speed, 29° Sch. Camera speed, 16 frames per second
Subject, normal. Filter, none.
For film at 26° Sch., open lens aperture by one whole stop.
For film at 32° Sch., close lens aperture by one whole stop.

Artificial Light

Angle of light	No. of lamps	Distance (lamp to subject) (ft.)			
		3	4½	6	9
0°–45° . .	1	f. 2·8	f. 1·9	f. 1·4	—
	2	f. 4	f. 2·8	f. 1·9	f. 1·4
45°–70° . .	1	f. 1·9	f. 1·4	—	—
	2	f. 2·8	f. 1·9	f. 1·4	—
70°–90° . .	1	f. 1·4	—	—	—
	2	f. 1·9	f. 1·4	—	—

Film speed, 30° to 31° Sch. Camera speed, 16 frames per second. Subject, normal. Filter, none. Lighting by Photofloods in good reflectors; surroundings, medium-light to light.

For film at 27° Sch., open lens aperture by one whole stop.

Note: Where two lamps are used, one can be one distance farther away than the other (e.g. one could be at 6 ft. and the other at 9 ft.) at the same angle; *or* one can be used at the next wider angle than the other (e.g. one could be used at 30° and the other at 60°) at the same distance. In either of these cases, the exposures given above will hold good.

Processing

When purchasing sub-standard ciné film, the cost of processing by the makers is frequently included in the price.

Except where the cinematographer has the considerable space, the necessary darkroom apparatus, and the many other facilities required for processing lengths of film up to at least 50 ft., it is recommended that all developing, etc., be done by firms who specialise in ciné-film processing.

Editing

Ciné film which has been processed will be found to require editing to some extent before it can be satisfactorily projected. The purpose of this editing is to remove (i) spoilt frames where the camera has stopped and started between shots, (ii) unexposed and blackened ends caused by loading and unloading, and (iii) material which is considered below standard. Further, it may be considered desirable to rearrange the shots into some better sequence and to introduce individual shots or sequences of shots by titles.

Cutting

The minimum requirements for successful cutting are a film splicer, a scraper, a supply of film cement and a brush. A refinement is a film viewer through which short lengths can be passed for inspection through a lens during cutting and splicing.

The important point to watch in splicing film is to so cut the film that, after splicing, the frames will run at the correct distances apart through the projector. If after any splice the frame is shown on the screen to be split, necessitating adjustment of the projector-gate, that splice is a bad one and should be remade.

Actual joining in the splicer is simple. One end of the film to be joined is located by its perforations in one side of the splicer and clamped in position emulsion side up. The small strip of emulsion left showing is scraped cleanly away, and the part of the film left bare is given a thin coat of cement. The other end of the film to be joined is now located (emulsion side up) by its perforations in the other side of the splicer and clamped down. In 30 to 60 seconds the cement is dry and the film may be removed from the splicer and any surplus cement carefully scraped away. Fuller directions will be found accompanying any film splicer bought.

When handling moderate lengths of film, the edited film may be spooled on to one of the projector reels, preferably the top reel with the frames upside down and the emulsion side inwards, ready for showing. If the lengths of film are likely to be large, a film rewinder is helpful.

Titling

It is accepted by most workers that unless titling is neat it is best left alone, such descriptions as may be necessary being given by the projectionist.

Titles are usually preferred as white lettering on a dark ground, and may be drawn by the editor if he is skilled in such work. Alternatively, apparatus may be purchased whereby cut letters can be arranged on a dark ground, being held in place either by slots or by the fact that the letters are magnetised.

The title set up, it must be photographed as a shot, the length of the shot to be the time it takes to read the title through twice fairly quickly, with a minimum of 3 seconds.

The above details also hold good if only single frames are to be edited into a sequence, as in the case of making film strip (see Lantern Plates, page 122).

PROJECTION

Projection Speed

THE general notes on projectors in the section on Lantern Slides should be studied. The essential difference between a still projector and a ciné projector is that the former has a slide carrier whereas the latter has mechanism similar to that found in the ciné camera (whereby the film is transported so that frames are positioned at the gate at the correct intervals, a moving shutter cutting off the light while the film is actually in motion).

It is usual to run a projector at a constant speed (16 frames per second for silent film; 24 frames per second for sound), fast and slow motion being achieved by regulation of the speed of taking in the camera. Some projectors have the facility of variable speed, however.

Flicker

It is found in practice that the human eye is conscious of flicker if a light is turned on and off at 16 or 24 times per second, but that it is not conscious of flicker if the light is turned on and off at about 50 times per second.

In silent projectors, therefore, the shutter is designed to cut off light three times per frame, once for film movement and twice more, giving a flicker-rate of 48 per second. In sound projectors the same flicker-rate is achieved by cutting off the light twice per frame, once for film movement and once more.

Projection Sizes

As in the case of Lantern Slides, the size of the projected picture depends primarily upon the size of the film frame, the focal length of the projector lens, and the length of throw.

The usual focal lengths of projector lenses are: for 16 mm., 2 in.; for 9·5 mm., 1½ in.; for 8 mm., 1 in. The following table, based on such focal lengths, gives the width of projected pictures for various distances of throw. Where a lens of focal length other than the ones named is used, or where the throw is of intermediate distance, size of projected picture may be worked out from the formula on page 121.

Throw	16 mm. (2-in. lens)	9·5 mm. (1½-in. lens)		8 mm. (1-in. lens)
	Silent and sound	Silent	Sound	Silent only
ft.	ft. in.	ft. in.	ft. in.	ft. in.
6	1 1	1 4	1 1	1 0
8	1 5	1 10	1 5	1 4
10	1 10	2 4	1 10	1 9
12	2 2	2 9	2 2	2 1
15	2 9	3 6	2 9	2 7
20	3 8	4 8	3 8	3 6
30	5 6	7 0	5 6	5 3
40	7 4	9 4	7 4	7 0
50	9 2	11 8	9 2	8 9

APPARATUS

Cameras

Name	Size	Lens	Int. lens	Speed (f.p.s.)	Max. loading (ft.)	Price group
B&H Autoload .	16	f. 1·9	Yes	16–64	50	D
B&H Sportster .	8	f. 2·5	Yes	16–64	25	C
B&H 70DA .	16	f. 1·9	Yes (T)	8–64	100	E
Ciné-Kodak 8–55	8	f. 2·7		16	25	B
Dekko Standard	9·5	f. 2·5	Yes	8–64	30	C
Dekko 110 .	8	f. 1·9	Yes	8–64	25	C
Dekko 128 .	8	f. 2·5	Yes	8–64	25	A
Paillard H16 .	16	f. 1·4	Yes (T)	8–64	100	E
Paillard L8 .	8	f. 1·9	Yes	12–32	25	D
Pathescope H .	9·5	f. 2·5		10–32	30	A

Abbreviations: f.p.s. = frames per second; T = interchangeable lenses in revolving turret; Prices Group A = £30–£40; B = £40–£50; C = £50–£60; D = £60–£100; E = Above £100.

Note: All the cameras in the above list in the 8-mm. size take Double-8 film.

Projectors

Name	Size (mm.)	Variable speed	Max. loading (ft.)	Illumination (watts)	Price group
Ampro Stylist*	16	Yes	2000	1000	C
B&H Screenmaster	8		400	400	B
Pathescope Son*	9·5	Yes	900	100	C
Pathescope Gem	9·5	Yes	900	100	A
Pathescope Gem	16	Yes	900	100	A
Specto 8	8		900	500	A
Specto 9·5	9·5		900	500	B
Specto 16	16		900	500	B
Specto Dual	9·5 & 16		900	500	B

* Sound projector (price includes loudspeaker, etc.). Price Group A = £30–40; B = £40–£65; C = Above £65.

Other Apparatus

For consistent results it is considered essential to have a reliable photo-electric exposure meter or an exposure photometer (see page 45). Further, although the depth of field of ciné-camera lenses is great, a good rangefinder (see page 42) will ensure well-focused close-ups.

If a tripod is to be used, it must be at least as rigid as that necessary for a 35-mm. still camera, and should have a pan-and-tilt head with handle for smooth camera movement. Notes on tripods appear on page 46.

A lens hood is desirable (see page 47), especially for occasions where strong light may strike across the surface of the camera lens.

Film Expenditure Table

Duration of shot (sec.)	9·5 and 16 mm.						8 mm.		
	Frames per second						Frames per second		
	8	12	16	24	32	48	8	16	32
2	$\frac{2}{5}$	$\frac{3}{5}$	$\frac{4}{5}$	$1\frac{1}{5}$	$1\frac{3}{5}$	$2\frac{2}{5}$	$\frac{1}{5}$	$\frac{2}{5}$	$\frac{4}{5}$
3	$\frac{3}{5}$	1	$1\frac{1}{5}$	$1\frac{4}{5}$	$2\frac{2}{5}$	$3\frac{3}{5}$	$\frac{1}{4}$	$\frac{3}{5}$	$1\frac{1}{5}$
4	$\frac{4}{5}$	$1\frac{1}{5}$	$1\frac{3}{5}$	$2\frac{2}{5}$	$3\frac{1}{5}$	$4\frac{4}{5}$	$\frac{2}{5}$	$\frac{4}{5}$	$1\frac{3}{5}$
5	1	$1\frac{1}{2}$	2	3	4	6	$\frac{1}{2}$	1	2
6	$1\frac{1}{5}$	$1\frac{4}{5}$	$2\frac{2}{5}$	$3\frac{3}{5}$	$4\frac{4}{5}$	$7\frac{1}{5}$	$\frac{3}{5}$	$1\frac{1}{5}$	$2\frac{2}{5}$
7	$1\frac{2}{5}$	2	$2\frac{4}{5}$	$4\frac{1}{5}$	$5\frac{3}{5}$	$8\frac{2}{5}$	$\frac{3}{4}$	$1\frac{2}{5}$	$2\frac{4}{5}$
8	$1\frac{3}{5}$	$2\frac{2}{5}$	$3\frac{1}{5}$	$4\frac{4}{5}$	$6\frac{2}{5}$	$9\frac{3}{5}$	$\frac{4}{5}$	$1\frac{3}{5}$	$3\frac{1}{5}$
9	$1\frac{4}{5}$	$2\frac{3}{4}$	$3\frac{3}{5}$	$5\frac{2}{5}$	$7\frac{1}{5}$	$10\frac{4}{5}$	1	$1\frac{4}{5}$	$3\frac{3}{5}$
10	2	3	4	6	8	12	1	2	4
11	$2\frac{1}{5}$	$3\frac{1}{4}$	$4\frac{2}{5}$	$6\frac{3}{5}$	$8\frac{4}{5}$	$13\frac{1}{5}$	1	$2\frac{1}{5}$	$4\frac{2}{5}$
12	$2\frac{2}{5}$	$3\frac{3}{5}$	$4\frac{4}{5}$	$7\frac{1}{5}$	$9\frac{3}{5}$	$14\frac{2}{5}$	$1\frac{1}{5}$	$2\frac{2}{5}$	$4\frac{4}{5}$
13	$2\frac{3}{5}$	4	$5\frac{1}{5}$	$7\frac{4}{5}$	$10\frac{2}{5}$	$15\frac{3}{5}$	$1\frac{1}{4}$	$2\frac{3}{5}$	$5\frac{1}{5}$
14	$2\frac{4}{5}$	$4\frac{1}{5}$	$5\frac{3}{5}$	$8\frac{2}{5}$	$11\frac{1}{5}$	$16\frac{4}{5}$	$1\frac{2}{5}$	$2\frac{4}{5}$	$5\frac{3}{5}$
15	3	$4\frac{1}{2}$	6	9	12	18	$1\frac{1}{2}$	3	6
16	$3\frac{1}{5}$	$4\frac{4}{5}$	$6\frac{2}{5}$	$9\frac{3}{5}$	$12\frac{4}{5}$	$19\frac{1}{5}$	$1\frac{3}{5}$	$3\frac{1}{5}$	$6\frac{2}{5}$
17	$3\frac{2}{5}$	5	$6\frac{4}{5}$	$10\frac{1}{5}$	$13\frac{3}{5}$	$20\frac{2}{5}$	$1\frac{3}{4}$	$3\frac{2}{5}$	$6\frac{4}{5}$
18	$3\frac{3}{5}$	$5\frac{2}{5}$	$7\frac{1}{5}$	$10\frac{4}{5}$	$14\frac{2}{5}$	$21\frac{3}{5}$	$1\frac{4}{5}$	$3\frac{3}{5}$	$7\frac{1}{5}$
19	$3\frac{4}{5}$	$5\frac{3}{4}$	$7\frac{3}{5}$	$11\frac{2}{5}$	$15\frac{1}{5}$	$22\frac{4}{5}$	2	$3\frac{4}{5}$	$7\frac{3}{5}$
20	4	6	8	12	16	24	2	4	8
25	5	$7\frac{1}{2}$	10	15	20	30	$2\frac{1}{2}$	5	10
30	6	9	12	18	24	36	3	6	12
35	7	$10\frac{1}{2}$	14	21	28	42	$3\frac{1}{2}$	7	14
40	8	12	16	24	32	48	4	8	16
45	9	$13\frac{1}{2}$	18	27	36	54	$4\frac{1}{2}$	9	18
50	10	15	20	30	40	60	5	10	20
60	12	18	24	36	48	72	6	12	24
75	15	$22\frac{1}{2}$	30	45	60	90	$7\frac{1}{2}$	15	30
100	20	30	40	60	80	120	10	20	40
min.									
2			48	72				24	
3			72	108				36	
4			96	144				48	
5			120	180				60	
10			240	360				120	
20			480	720				240	
30			720	1080				360	

Depth of Field Tables

Distances are in feet and inches. Use $f.$ 1·9 distances for any larger stop. Where no second distance is shown, the second distance is understood to be ∞.

$12\frac{1}{2}$-mm. ($\frac{1}{2}$-in.) Lens

Distance focused (ft.)	Stop						
	1·9	2·8	4	5·6	8	11	16
2	1 : 10 2 : 2	1 : 9 2 : 4	1 : 8 2 : 6	1 : 8 3 : 0	1 : 7 3 : 6	1 : 6 5 : 0	1 : 5 ∞
3	2 : 9 3 : 6	2 : 6 3 : 9	2 : 3 4 : 3	2 : 1 5 : 6	1 : 11 8 : 0	1 : 8 12 : 0	1 : 6 ∞
4	3 : 5 5 : 0	3 : 2 5 : 6	2 : 10 6 : 8	2 : 8 8 : 0	2 : 4 20 : 0	2 : 0 ∞	1 : 8 ∞
6	4 : 9 8 : 4	4 : 3 10 : 0	3 : 9 15 : 0	3 : 4 30 : 0	2 : 9 ∞	2 : 3 ∞	1 : 10 ∞
10	6 : 9 19 : 0	6 : 0 30 : 0	5 : 3 ∞	4 : 4 ∞	3 : 4 ∞	2 : 8 ∞	2 : 1 ∞
15	8 : 9 52 : 6	7 : 6 ∞	6 : 0 ∞	5 : 0 ∞	3 : 9 ∞	3 : 3 ∞	2 : 4 ∞
25	11 : 0	9 : 6	7 : 0	6 : 0	4 : 3	3 : 6	2 : 5
Inf.	20 : 9	15 : 0	10 : 6	7 : 6	5 : 3	3 : 9	2 : 7

20-mm. ($\frac{3}{4}$-in.) Lens

Distance focused (ft.)	Stop						
	1·9	2·8	4	5·6	8	11	16
2	1 : 10 2 : 2	1 : 10 2 : 2	1 : 9 2 : 3	1 : 9 2 : 4	1 : 8 2 : 7	1 : 6 3 : 0	1 : 6 ∞
3	2 : 9 3 : 4	2 : 8 3 : 5	2 : 7 3 : 8	2 : 5 4 : 0	2 : 2 4 : 9	2 : 0 6 : 0	1 : 9 ∞
4	3 : 6 4 : 7	3 : 5 4 : 10	3 : 3 5 : 3	3 : 0 6 : 0	2 : 8 8 : 0	2 : 5 12 : 0	2 : 2 ∞
6	5 : 0 7 : 3	4 : 9 8 : 0	4 : 5 9 : 3	4 : 0 12 : 0	3 : 5 24 : 0	3 : 0 ∞	2 : 4 ∞

20-mm. (¾-in.) Lens (continued)

Distance focused (ft.)	Stop						
	1·9	2·8	4	5·6	8	11	16
10	7 : 9 14 : 3	7 : 0 17 : 0	6 : 4 24 : 0	5 : 6 60 : 0	4 : 9 ∞	3 : 9 ∞	2 : 10 ∞
15	10 : 6 27 : 0	9 : 3 40 : 0	8 : 0 ∞	6 : 8 ∞	5 : 3 ∞	4 : 3 ∞	3 : 2 ∞
25	14 : 6 94 : 0	12 : 0 ∞	10 : 0 ∞	8 : 0 ∞	6 : 0 ∞	4 : 10 ∞	3 : 6 ∞
Inf.	33 : 6	24 : 0	16 : 9	12 : 0	8 : 6	6 : 0	4 : 3

25-mm. (1-in.) Lens

Distance focused (ft.)	Stop						
	1·9	2·8	4	5·6	8	11	16
2	1 : 11 2 : 1	1 : 10 2 : 2	1 : 10 2 : 2	1 : 9 2 : 4	1 : 8 2 : 6	1 : 7 2 : 9	1 : 5 3 : 3
3	2 : 10 3 : 3	2 : 9 3 : 4	2 : 7 3 : 6	2 : 6 3 : 9	2 : 4 4 : 2	2 : 2 5 : 0	1 : 11 7 : 0
4	3 : 8 4 : 5	3 : 6 4 : 7	3 : 4 5 : 0	3 : 2 5 : 6	2 : 11 6 : 6	2 : 7 8 : 6	2 : 3 17 : 0
6	5 : 3 7 : 0	5 : 0 7 : 6	4 : 8 8 : 6	4 : 3 10 : 0	3 : 10 14 : 0	3 : 4 30 : 0	2 : 9 ∞
10	8 : 2 13 : 0	7 : 6 15 : 0	6 : 9 19 : 0	6 : 0 30 : 0	5 : 0 ∞	4 : 3 ∞	3 : 6 ∞
15	11 : 3 23 : 0	10 : 0 30 : 0	8 : 9 55 : 0	7 : 6 ∞	6 : 0 ∞	5 : 0 ∞	4 : 0 ∞
25	16 : 0 58 : 0	13 : 6 ∞	11 : 6 ∞	9 : 6 ∞	7 : 6 ∞	5 : 9 ∞	4 : 6 ∞
Inf.	44 : 0	30 : 0	21 : 0	15 : 0	10 : 6	7 : 6	5 : 3

Part Six

COLOUR PHOTOGRAPHY

COLOUR SYSTEMS

N O SPECIAL apparatus is necessary for making colour photographs, except that some special filters may be required, as described later. In general, any reliable camera will produce good colour photographs, the main requirements being that the shutter-speeds are fairly accurate and that the lens is of good quality.

Apart from apparatus, the great difference between black-and-white and colour photography is in technique: in the former there is some room for error in the various processes before a picture becomes so bad as to be unacceptable, but in the latter there is little or none.

There are two basic types of colour photographs: the transparency (for viewing by transmitted light) and the colour print (for viewing by reflected light, as in the case of black-and-white prints).

The Transparency

The production of a transparency depends upon the fact that if the three colours red, green and blue are viewed together by transmitted light, the result will be white, and that if any of these colours are omitted or modified in strength, there can be produced in the result any colour as seen in nature. As a practical example of this principle, there is a type of colour-negative material (Dufaycolor) in which the three colours mentioned above are placed upon a plate or film as a "reseau" or network of great fineness: this reseau is in company with a negative emulsion which is exposed through the colours. In effect the reseau acts as a set of filters spread finely and with great evenness over the plate or film, each tiny portion of which will admit light to the emulsion in

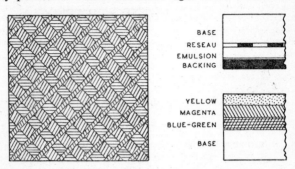

BASE
RESEAU
EMULSION
BACKING

YELLOW
MAGENTA
BLUE-GREEN
BASE

COLOUR PHOTOGRAPHY SYSTEMS

On the left is the arrangement of the reseau in Dufaycolor —continuous bands of red superimposed on alternate bands of blue and green. At top right is shown the placing of the reseau, exposure being through the base.

Bottom right: a non-reseau material whose layers are selectively developed.

accordance with its properties (see Filters, page 34). When the plate or film is suitably processed and examined by holding it up to a light of the same quality as that by which it was made (daylight, say), a colour picture will be seen which is a reproduction of the subject originally photographed, the developed emulsion passing or holding back various parts of the red, green and blue reseau in suitable proportions. This is a somewhat over-simplified explanation, and for fuller details the reader is referred to the *Dufaycolor Data Book* published by the makers of the material.

The reseau, by its very nature, stops some of the transmitted light passing through the transparency, and for that reason reseau-type material is not considered so good for projection as material in which there is no reseau.

In this material, the plate or film has three layers of emulsion. The top layer accepts blue light, the middle layer green and the bottom layer red; and when the material is exposed to a coloured subject its layers will be affected according to the components of the various subject-colours they "see." Upon development and reversal to positive, the plate or film is a combination of three black-and-white images, each image being that of one of the three colours. The next process is to selectively dye these images, the colours of the dyes being complementary to the original colour-sensitivities of the respective layers. Thus the blue-sensitive layer will accept only a yellow dye, the green-sensitive only a red dye, and the red-sensitive layer only a blue dye. As the final stage in the process, the black-and-white images on the respective layers are dissolved away, leaving only the dyes in combination to reproduce the colours of the original subject. Again this is an over-simplified explanation, and the reader is referred to the literature published by the various makers of colour material for further information.

It should be noted here, however, that in the first process mentioned the black-and-white image and the reseau are left on the plate or film; and in the second process the black-and-white image is removed and there is no reseau. Most workers in the field of colour prefer the second process, even though the processing procedure is more complicated.

Colour Prints

This system is somewhat similar to black-and-white photography inasmuch that the first stage is the production of a negative, and that the final result is a print which is viewed by reflected light.

The negative is a colour transparency with all three colours complementary to the colour of the original subject: e.g. flesh colours are blue-green and a blue sky is yellowish. In brief, the colours are themselves "negative" in much the same way that tones are "negative" (e.g. blacks are white and whites are black) in black-and-white negatives. The printing process reverses the colour negative to a colour positive—i.e. a colour print—the processes being somewhat similar to those described in the selective-dyeing method above.

Black-and-White Prints

Where an ordinary positive colour-transparency has been made, a black-and-white print can be taken from it by one of two methods.

In the first method, a black-and-white negative is made from the transparency by contact or projection (care being taken that no stray light escapes from the enlarger), the material for making this negative being slow panchromatic of fine grain. This negative, developed and fixed in the ordinary way, is then used for the making of prints by the usual black-and-white procedure.

In the second method, a special positive panchromatic paper is used. It is exposed to the colour transparency by contact or projection, developed, reversed and fixed. The process of reversal is similar to that described later, and for further information the reader is referred to the directions issued by the makers of the special paper to be used.

ACHIEVING CORRECT COLOUR

Colour Temperature

IN colour photography the colour of the light by which a picture is taken is of considerable importance. If a subject is lit with yellow, the result will be predominantly yellow; if the subject is lit with red, the result will be predominantly red. Disregard of this broad rule is largely responsible for the disappointment many photographers have expressed in the general appearance of their colour pictures.

Unfortunately the human eye is very tolerant of the colour of light sources, while it is not tolerant of colour-aberrations in photography. For example, the human eye will see a blue sky as blue, but will accept anything lit entirely by that light as white. Similarly at night, the human eye will accept the light coming from a new tungsten lamp as white, whereas the light contains a high proportion of yellow. Some means of estimating the colour of light is necessary if that light is to be used successfully in colour photography.

This estimation is achieved by means of colour-temperature,

arrived at in this way: if a piece of black carbon is heated sufficiently, it will glow red; if heated more the glow will become yellow; still more, and it will glow blue-white. If one expresses light in terms of the temperature necessary to heat the carbon in order to produce that light, one has a ready means of measuring colour-temprature.

In the following table is a rough indication of colour-temperatures, expressed in degrees Kelvin (°K.), a scale which is based upon the "absolute temperature zero" or minus 273° Centigrade.

Colour Temperature Table

Source of light	Colour temp. (°K.)	Remarks
25-watt tungsten* . .	2500	Too yellow for type "A"
100-watt tungsten* . Flashbulbs (yellow) .	2900	Correct for type "A"
Photoflood . . .	3400	Too blue for type "A", too yellow for type "D"
Flashbulbs (clear) . .	4000	do.
Sunlight, pale sky . Electronic flashtube . Flashbulbs (blue) .	6000	Correct for type "D"
Sunlight, blue sky . .	7000 to 15,000	Too blue for type "D"

* When lamp is new. Colour tends to become progressively yellower as lamp ages.

"A" =colour material suitable for artificial light.
"D" =colour material suitable for daylight.

Filters

It will be deduced from the above table that there are two principal types of colour material made: for 2900°K. (corres-
10

ponding to 100-watt tungsten lighting) and for 6000°K. (corresponding to sunny day conditions). The first type is generally labelled "A" for artificial light (but see table and notes below); the second type "D" for daylight.

If colour material is used for any other light than that for which it is made, a filter must be used over the lens of the camera in order to correct the colour-temperature of the light passing to the emulsion.

It will further be seen from the table that daylight itself is by no means consistent in colour-temperature, and that sunlight from a blue sky needs correction, or the resulting picture will have an overtone of blue. The correction filter used in this case is a very pale yellow, and should be of a type advised by the makers of the colour material used.

Makers also advise upon the correct filters to use when using an "A"-type material in daylight or photoflood, or a "D"-type material in tungsten light or photoflood. These special filters are pale yellow, blue, yellow-brown or pink of varying densities, and have factors ranging from ×1½ to ×4.

Colour Material

Most colour material is film. Colour plates are usually obtainable on special order.

Material		For	Available in	Speed (Sch.)	Processed by
Agfacolor K	.	A	35, RF	24°	M, D & P, User
Agfacolor T	.	D	35, RF	24°	do.
Dufaycolor D	.	D	35, RF	21°	do.
Dufaycolor T	.	A	CF	22°	do.
Ektachrome	.	D	RF, CF	22°	do.
Ektachrome B	.	A	CF	22°	do.
Gevacolour	.	D	35	22°	do.
Gevacolour	.	A	35	22°	do.
Ilford D	.	D	35	24°	Makers only
Ilford A	.	P	35	24°	do.
Kodacolor*	.	D	RF	26°	do.
Kodacolor*	.	P	RF	26°	do.
Kodachrome	.	D	35, B	22°	do.
Kodachrome A	.	P	35, B	22°	do.

Notes: The speed is the speed of the material; allowance must be made for any filter used.

The speed of colour-material is expressed in the same way as the speed of black-and-white material, and following our practice hitherto the speeds in the table opposite are given in terms of European Scheiner.

* For making colour prints; all other materials listed above are for making positive transparencies.

A = Artificial light (Tungsten, 2900°K.); D = Daylight (6000°K.); P = Artificial light (Photoflood, 3400°K.).

35 = 35-mm. material; RF = Roll film; CF = Cut film; B = Bantam (size 88, 828). M = Makers; D & P = Developing and Printing agencies.

Exposure

It has already been mentioned that while there is some room for error in black-and-white photography before the results become unacceptable, in colour photography there is very little.

This applies particularly to exposure. Colour material must be regarded as having no exposure-latitude, and consequently every effort must be made to determine exposure with accuracy.

Under simple lighting conditions—such as sunlight from a pale sky in the open, or tungsten of known wattage at measured distances—the determination of exposure by calculator will give good results; but in any other lighting conditions—i.e. daylight in shadow, or complex artificial lighting—a reliable exposure meter should be used.

It has further been mentioned that the human eye accepts as white much that is not white, and this fact must be taken into account when making colour pictures. The principal difficulty is reflection. As a simple example, supposing it is desired to make colour pictures of a young woman in a garden. In the first picture the model is sitting upon a lawn, and in the result it will be found that her complexion is flesh colour tinged with varying tones of green—the lawn has reflected its colour into her face, although such reflection was not noticed by eye. Again, in the second picture the model is stooping to smell a mass of fine red roses, and in the result

her complexion is found to be heavily tinged with red—
the blooms have reflected their colour into her face.

This reflection may be said to be everywhere in some degree.
It becomes apparent to the eye in the child's game of holding
a buttercup to the chin, when the flower reflects a perceptible
patch of yellow on to the skin.

The first rule of making colour photographs must be,
therefore, to see that no masses of strong colour are so near
to pale surfaces that the one will degrade the other.

Contrast

In black-and-white photography good contrast is achieved
by ensuring that tones of grey are sufficiently varied to give
a distinct and harmonious result. To this end, black-and-
white negative materials are given a fairly long range for tone-
separation. In colour materials there are no varying tones
of grey, and the range for tone-separation is much shorter.

The effect is twofold: agreeable contrast can be achieved
in the main only by the placing of colours in the subject, and
shadow areas in colour materials come out much darker than
they do on black-and-white materials.

Because of all this, the colour masses in the subject should
not be too pronounced, and certainly two strong colour masses
of great difference should not be placed close to one another.
Further, the light falling upon the subject should be even and
well diffused: so far as daylight is concerned, the best light
is considered to be sunlight well broken down by slight haze.

It is the placing of colour areas, and not areas of highlight
and shadow, which will give acceptable contrast in colour
photographs.

Finally, the operator should remember that most colour
material tends to render colours a little more brilliantly than
in nature, and that strong colour contrasts which are striking
to the eye might appear merely gaudy on a transparency.

Processing

Only a broad outline of processing technique can be given
here, for each make of material has its own formulæ and
routine. It will be noted from the list of colour material

given earlier that with some makes processing can be done by the makers only.

It is strongly recommended that the processing of colour material should be attempted only by those photographers who have had a considerable experience in the accurate processing of black-and-white materials. The formulæ, times, temperatures and routines given by the makers in their directions should be very strictly followed.

Development is basically a reversal process in which a negative is first obtained; then the negative image is bleached out and a positive one developed in, and (in non-reseau material) selectively dyed. Since accuracy in timing of first development is essential, a stop bath is frequently used after this stage; and since the processes cover a fair length of time and the emulsion tends to become rather soft and easily damaged, it is usual to immerse the material in a hardening bath between each stage. Washing and rinsing of the material is frequent; they generally take place after the stop bath, after bleaching, after each hardening, and after all stages of processing have been completed. The time required for all stages varies from 45 min. to $1\frac{1}{4}$ hr. according to the make of material used.

Colour Faults

Some of the faults which may be apparent in colour transparencies have already been indicated in the preceding pages. In the main they take the form of degraded colours due to the use of incorrect material for the light by which the pictures were made, the reflection of colour from one surface to another, and the placing together of strong colour-masses in the subject. For the last two of these there is no remedy, although some improvement may possibly be effected by viewing through a suitable filter; in the first, binding up the transparency with suitable filter material will generally give correction.

Some other faults are listed overleaf, and it should be noted here that, except in the two instances stated, the correction of faults in colour material is practically impossible.

The user of colour should always bear in mind that his materials are expensive; hence every possible effort should be made to ensure correct exposure.

Colour Faults Chart

Fault	Cause
Transparency dark; no detail in shadows	Under-exposure
Transparency dark; some detail in shadows	Insufficient first development. *Remedy* (for reseau only, if fault slight), reduce gently in ferricyanide (page 92)
Transparency light; pale, wash-ed-out colours	Over-exposure or excessive first development *Remedy* (for reseau only, if fault slight), bleach and redevelop as directed by makers of material
Some colours show better detail than others	Camera lens uncorrected and not suitable for colour photography
No colour	Incorrect order of processing; or (reseau) material placed in camera back-to-front; i.e. with emulsion instead of reseau facing lens
Colours as complementaries (i.e. transparency is a colour negative and not a colour positive)	Incorrect order of processing

VIEWING COLOUR

Light

JUST AS the colour temperature of light is an important consideration in taking colour pictures, so it is an important consideration when viewing them.

The usual rule is that colour transparencies should be viewed in diffused daylight, and some idea of the importance of correct viewing light can be obtained by holding a transparency up to a white cloud and then up to a patch of blue sky. Where it is intended that the transparencies are to be

viewed almost entirely by artificial light—e.g. by projection
on to a screen (see section on Lantern Plates)—then some
modification is possible, for the use of filters, either at the
time the transparency is made or at the time it is viewed, will
give correct colour rendering. Directions given by the makers
of the colour material used should be consulted in this
connection.

Dealing with the general tone of a colour transparency, if
after all precautions have been taken it is found that a transparency has degraded colour, the matter may be put right for
viewing by binding up the transparency with a suitable layer
of filter material. As a simple example, supposing a transparency has been taken in daylight and that, owing to the
strength of the blue sky, there is apparent an overall blueness;
the fault may be corrected by binding up the transparency
with a very pale-yellow filter. In the same way, if a transparency suitable for viewing by diffused daylight is examined
by artificial light it will appear somewhat yellow, and the
yellowness may be dispersed by interposing a very pale-blue
filter between the transparency and the viewing light.

(*Note:* These filter colours are given as examples only; they
may not be correct for different makes of material. For
example, some materials would require a pinkish or yellowish-
brown filter in the first case, and a mauve-blue in the second.
The literature of the makers should be consulted.)

Viewing Devices

Transparencies may be viewed by simply holding up to the
light, as already indicated. For best results, however, they
are best seen through a viewer or by projection.

Whichever way they are to be viewed, it is recommended
that they be bound up as indicated in the section on Lantern
Slides, otherwise damage from repeated handling is practically
inevitable.

Viewers are devices which consist essentially of a means
for holding a transparency, and a lens for examining it. The
viewer may be made to hold up to the light, or it may contain
within a small lamp-house a source of artificial light.
The usual sizes of such viewers are: 24×36 mm. and 2 in.
square.

Projectors are precisely the same in type and size as has

been described in the section on Lantern Plates. With regard to screens, it is held by some workers that a flat, matt-white surface is best for colour; the beaded type, it is thought, has a tendency to exaggerate the colours somewhat. The final choice is a matter for individual taste.

INDEX

94 7